VIOLENCE EVERY SUNDAY

Also by Bill McSweeny
GO UP FOR GLORY

(with Bill Russell)

VIOLENCE

The Story of a

by MIKE HOLOVAK

Coach of the Boston Patriots

EVERY SUNDAY

Professional Football Coach

and BILL McSWEENY

Coward-McCann, Inc. New York

To:

The football widow, Edith; and the football daughters, Michele and Terrie; and to all those I have known throughout these years, the opponents and the teammates and the players; and to Billy Sullivan and the Boston Patriots' owners; and for any man or boy who has ever held a football and dreamed.

The authors wish to acknowledge a special debt of thanks to Thomas G. Feenan of H. P. Hood and Sons, who conceived the idea of this book and without whom it would not have been possible.

Contents

Foreword

This is the story of both twenty-five years of football and the formation of the National and American Football Leagues.

It is written during one specific season, 1966, as the Boston Patriots chase the Buffalo Bills for the Eastern Division championship.

When I began, I wanted more than anything else to bring you into a world which I have loved many seasons.

I also wanted to provide a full understanding of the professional game.

Therefore, this book is in two sections. It seems strange to me to say it, but the past twenty-five years are all history now. So this opening half is written in the past tense and peopled with those whom I have known—the national championship teams at Boston College; Leahy; the bowl teams, Sugar, Cotton and Orange; the professionals and the National Football League in a postward period when the sport was still not fully recognized; Papa Bear Halas and Sid Luckman, Waterfield and Harmon, and all the others.

Then there were the college days, coaching at Boston College and finally the formation of the American Football League.

Next comes the second half, written in the present tense. This season. My season. The intrigues, the difficulties, the soaring heights reached when we win; the inches and the

11

bounces and, finally, the big one against Joe Willie Namath at Shea Stadium with 30,000,000 watching their television sets and 60,000 cheering, and the Super Bowl at the end of the rainbow.

They are here in these pages, past and present. I hope that in reading it, you will discover why some of us stay in this sport for life; why, even though we are professionals, the sport is more a disease and a joy than a method of making money.

At the same time, I hope you will learn from it of the rogues and the charmers and the fighters and the furious challenge of the slick ones and the slackers, and of the nagging pressures.

This is exactly the way it was this year and in my lifetime. The participants were not all good, nor were they all bad. Just people, doing the best they could in an occupation which is a miniscule part of the American culture, except on Sunday afternoons when half a nation watches.

Always on Sunday.

We die by the inches.

Michael J. Holovak
Boston, December 7, 1966

VIOLENCE EVERY SUNDAY

1.

The Long Bomb

NEW GUINEA lay off to port. Green. Lush. Dangerous. Filthy. Filled with death and people to make it.

I was feeling like a million dollars standing at the con of the PT boat with the dawn just raising the strange, soft, lush rose-purple of the Southwest Pacific.

I was a combat man now and never again would I be anything less. I had been out there and heard the sound of the guns and seen the bright, winking, white-hot lights of the 20 millimeters. It was my boat and the skipper was sleeping down below and the patrol was over and we were heading back to the base.

I held her steady at twenty knots, slightly left in the wake of the lead boat and I was the greatest man in the world, a USNR Ensign coming home from his first patrol with his hand on the helm.

Then the Jap came out of nowhere, flat on the deck and over the ridge-line, out of the hills with the rising sun at his back and who-whoom to port and w-w-w-h-h-aammmm to starboard and water rising and falling and the boat shuddering a little as the shrapnel sludged her plywood and the plane—a "Zeke"—was gone into a long spiraling climb for altitude and I was yelling down the hatch to wake the skipper, Joe Ellicott.

The skipper said, "I didn't need you to wake me up, Mr. Holovak. I heard the noise."

15

PT-131 held station. The Jap came back to look us over and we chased him off with the guns from both boats and in the hot sun of the morning we finally docked back at Itapi.

Wally Lemm had PT-114 in Squadron 8 and was in from Finchaven for a briefing. He kidded me about it. "Well," he said, "all you Pennsylvania hard-rocks are thick in the head. Here it is October third, the start of the football season, and you're falling asleep letting Japs take pot shots at you."

"Wally," I said, "I've always wondered how I'd react to the first combat patrol. Now I know. Scared as hell."

But I was proud. It was a long time ago and I was a young kid then and there were a lot of things we were still going to do in those plywood boats and a lot of places to go and a lot of things to remember. But I was proud that I had made a different kind of team and I guess if there is any one place where you can measure it up and say this is where it started, then this must be the place . . . off the coast of New Guinea, coming home in the breaking dawn, letting my dreams wander while a "Zeke" nearly put his own kind of football in my hip pocket.

I was thinking of that for the first time in years as I started this book. It is twenty-three years ago now and Sunday— December 11—I will be in Houston trying to beat the Oilers and close in on a championship.

Wally Lemm coaches the Houston Oilers now. It is a long time since I transferred to his boat as exec. It is a long time since he was invalided home and I became skipper. It is a longer time since the days when we were first in the Navy and he was one of those who stood up for me when I married Edith.

Here we are, a quarter of a century later, and I am going to go down there and do everything I can to beat him, and he will do everything he can to cost me a championship that everyone said I would never win anyway.

Maybe he will. But I doubt it. Because I am going to kick his brains in and outthink him. Then I am coming back to New York the following week and show Joe Namath that just to be able to throw a football isn't enough.

And after that? Kansas City and then the National Football League, and Vince Lombardi and Green Bay.

Because that is the way it is in my business. Every man's hand is against you and every week is life and death. A crazy miniature war is always being fought, a war that is really never going to end, a war that seeps deeply inside and you can't rid yourself of. It's like dope or drinking or smoking, I guess. You know it is inevitably going to kill you.

I know most certainly that one day I am just going to fall over dead from a heart attack.

But the fever is in my blood and that is just the way it is going to have to be.

These pages are full of the story of that fever and the fever in the blood of many men.

Football.

Football for money.

Football for pride.

Football for marbles.

We'll play it for any stakes. Once the game is in the man, it really doesn't matter anymore. He'll play even with a short bankroll, just to be in on the action.

The one thing I never expected was to write about it. Basically I am a most colorless character. At least, that's what the sportswriters sometimes say about me.

I'm sure nothing would have ever been done, if it hadn't been for Tom Feenan, of H.P. Hood and Sons, who had the original idea.

When it was decided, I made one point clear. This book is exactly the way football is and has been. I've never read a football book, but I can imagine some of them. I'll pass that pleasure up. They're about some good guys—and some bad guys—and they tell what the good guy or the bad guy wants you to know.

This one tells everything I can think of about me, ranging from when I was a kid through all the wild, crazy years of playing and through the beginnings of the American Football League.

I think it's honest.

When I began, I needed a jumping-off point. I guess the best place is right now. The Boston Patriots have just taken the Eastern Division lead of the American Football League. We beat Buffalo last Sunday and now we have to win two games—against Lemm at Houston Sunday and against Namath at New York a week from Sunday.

If we win or tie, then we win the Eastern Division title. If we win the title, then we play Kansas City. If we beat Kansas City, then we play in the first Super Bowl game.

Come along and we'll see what it is like to play pro football in modern America where the television eye is supposed to tell you everything.

Well, they don't let TV inside your uniform, anyway. So I'll give you a different view. Sort of an isolated camera focusing from inside a set of shoulder pads.

Watch out for the blind side blocks.

2.

The Gravedigger

IT STARTED WHEN I was a gravedigger in Lansford, Pennsylvania, a town where the only thing big was a coal mine.

I was born there on the first day of the 1919 football season —September 9th. Rockne was coaching Frank Leahy at Notre Dame.

My father—who died twenty-nine years ago—worked in the mine until it shut down. Then he went to work for a church where part of the job was digging graves. Actually, that's where Frank Leahy found me. My father was dead and I was supporting my mother by working out Dad's contract. Maybe it should make you fatalistic, digging graves. Maybe. It didn't make me that way. I still die a thousand deaths every Sunday afternoon.

Those days were different, though. I was just a big "Hunky" kid like you hear about. They say these kids were so tough that they used to chew nails. That might be an exaggeration.

Certainly, a lot of them made it to the pros, including my own quarterback, Babe Parilli, and Joe Namath. I don't think there are any better.

As for me, I was pretty lousy. I had four brothers and a sister, and my brothers were all really good players. There was Pete, who played at Fordham with the "Seven Blocks of

19

Granite," Charles, now a retired Navy captain, who played at the Naval Academy, John and Andy.

If the war hadn't come along, Pete probably would have made it in the pros. He became a navigator instead, and one day when we came back off patrol dropping some commandos behind the lines in New Britain, there was a letter.

It said, "Too bad about Pete."

Pete's B-17 was bombing Tarawa. It was shot down. That was all I ever was able to find out.

Gee, he really was a great football player.

Of course, that's getting ahead of the story, but it does all tie in together. Pete played at Fordham when Jim Crowley was the head coach and Frank Leahy was the line coach.

Leahy came down to Pennsylvania looking for hard-rocks in the anthracite region. I had graduated from high school with what might charitably be called passing marks and now I was plying my trade digging graves and making the collection on Sundays.

Dad had died when I was a senior, but I still had an itch to play football, so I worked out with the high school team. All I had was a helmet, no pads, but Ken Miller was the coach and he put up with me. He's now the freshman coach at the University of Pennsylvania. Miller thought I might have a chance and tipped off Jack Fish, the coach at Seton Hall prep, and I was given a chance to go to school.

In those days, going away to school was something really to consider carefully. The mines had reopened and there was plenty of work. My mother had never seen a football game, but football had been good to my brothers, and she finally told me to make my own decision.

Well, I was up there on the side of the hill digging a grave one day and thought it all over very carefully and decided I'd take a chance.

I'd never been outside of Pennsylvania in my life, but off I went—a "Hunky" coal miner-gravedigger—to Seton Hall, and my luck began running true. A dentist named Doctor Nork, who was the brother of Shenandoah High coach Bobby Nork, guided us Pennsylvania kids through Seton Hall and we were invited to meet Leahy at his house. Joe Repko, who later played at B.C., went with me.

I wish that I could describe this first meeting as something special, but it really wasn't. Everyone knew about Fordham and Jim Crowley, but Leahy was only an assistant. He didn't promise us a thing. Just wanted to know if we would play football for him.

I stress that because later on Leahy was accused of nineteen different kinds of double cross, including taking all the talent he scouted for Fordham to Boston College when he won the job. When he left B.C. they claimed he took it all to Notre Dame.

I can't speak for anyone but myself. Leahy never specifically mentioned the school. In fact, I wasn't too desperately interested in Fordham, since like any kid I didn't want to live in my brother Pete's shadow. Leahy wasn't the only one coming around. Repko and I had a good season at Seton Hall and we were All Metropolitan and getting some other offers—Villanova, Boston College, Georgetown, Manhattan. Schools that were big; schools that were growing.

We took some campus trips. We were young and cocky and there was one team we beat which was supposed to be pretty good, St. Cecilia's. Vince Lombardi was the coach. I hope you'll hear more about him in the last chapter of this book.

Two weeks later Leahy was back and asked us if we would play at B.C. There were five of us. Only Repko and I stayed. The rest were homesick.

Remember this—it was long before the days of the big bonus. Now, you hear about kids getting all kinds of gifts. I got conversation. Would I go to B.C.? Why not? I wasn't going anyplace anyway. What's wrong with Boston?

I'd never been farther north than New York City and in point of fact we weren't even invited up to see the B.C. campus. In the spring Leahy came by with Ed McKeever— you might remember that name, he plays a part in this book—and they looked at my muscles.

Holovak as a football
player at Boston Col-
lege

I don't know whether they liked them or not. The next thing I knew they were getting me a summer job working on a road gang outside Sing Sing and living in a Y.M.C.A. in White Plains, New York.

I wasn't complaining—it was at least a step up from grave-digging—and actually I requested hard labor to toughen me up.

In September we were at Boston College, getting that good Leahy training.

Call it cannon fodder.

Leahy put us up in a boarding house at 1933 Commonwealth Avenue with the most wonderful woman in the world, Nora "Noni" Moore. We lived there for four years—Repko, Charlie O'Rourke, Gene Goodreault, Freddie Naumetz, Mario "Yo-Yo" Gianelli and I.

Having provided such good accommodations, Leahy now put us out on our own. The name of the game was "Kill the Freshmen." If you couldn't kill them on the field, then kill then with the studies. No one gave you anything at Boston College.

Which was perfect. There are many things which can be said about football today. Some good, some bad. You get what you pay for in some conferences. In those days, the schools gave little, demanded a lot and—surprise—all the athletes weren't as big and stupid as their shoulder pads made them look.

The important thing with Leahy—and I think the important thing in all athletics and a good lesson to learn—was that his players were forced to prove themselves. Leahy gave his men a confidence which would last them all their lives. No man came to any of his teams with the guarantee that he would make it. No man competed without giving everything he had in himself.

As a result, when the rosters are checked, it is often discovered that his players went on to accomplish many things in worlds other than sports.

Cannon fodder? Certainly. But solid cannon fodder, a cannon fodder that learned the hard way, developed, proved itself and became, in truth, men. Men first, then players.

I was supposed to be a halfback, but I was the lousiest passer in the history of the single wing. The worst. Would you believe even worse than that? Freshman coach Ted Galligan worked patiently with me and, ultimately, developed me into a fullback. In those days this could be best described as "three yards and a cloud of dust." The dust—some wise guy said—came from Holovak's head.

During the summer I was turned over to McKeever. Ed was then the most popular man in football. He was great on fundamentals. All summer he treated me like any other clean-cut American boy. He put me out on the road gang to work on construction and threw the ball to me, taught me hand-offs, and knocked me down until I learned to block.

This was playing in the Leahy school, which provided nothing but a scholarship, some books and a hard time. Some coaches talk about character building, but Leahy was a practitioner of it.

Of course, he had some characters, too. He held random bed checks and the only ones he would catch in would be me and him. And I wasn't always sure about him.

Leahy came to B.C. for one reason—to win. His first year as a head coach was my first year. I saw him twice. He was busy building a bowl team. And he did it. B.C. lost only one game and went to the Cotton Bowl. I didn't see the game. Leahy didn't take freshmen. With him, it was always only the best. The others had to work for it.

Frankly, I saw nothing wrong with this. Nor did anyone else. This was in the period when a Leahy would put in his apprenticeship with a Crowley at Fordham, then catch a head coaching job, following in the footsteps of someone like the Iron Major—Frank Cavanaugh.

I'm pretty religious. In fact, very. At the same time I'm sure that the Jesuits will forgive me if I say that they prefer to play football as they teach life—to win. They had the winner in Leahy. He was young, scrappy, tough, brilliant. He surrounded himself with winners. Every assistant coach was great. Ever player was forced to drive himself to the limit of his potential. If you failed, then Leahy was there to say something caustic. One day a back lay on the ground. He had missed a pattern, failed to pick up his blocker, was lying there stunned by a tackler. The fans stood silently as the trainer rushed out and a worried referee hovered near by. Was it time for stretcher-bearers? No. Out came Leahy.

He looked down with disdain.

"Throw some dirt on him and let's get on with the game," he said.

The back continued to play. He may have been afraid to go to the bench.

Leahy was always Leahy. I make this point clear because he was the most famous man of his generation of coaches. He brought the T-formation to college football. If you're old enough to remember those days, then he challenged your imagination for years. If you played for him, he was absolutely loyal to you. If you had an idea, he listened. He was a superb football coach and has been my friend for years, yet, at one time, he cost me the only football coaching job I had. He very nearly made me a complete failure at the age of thirty-eight.

Or perhaps it was the fans of the Leahy mystique that made the Leahy legend. An interesting commentary, really, on the coaching profession. Leahy came to Boston College and created two straight bowl teams. Anyone who ever came after Leahy was automatically confronted with the ghost of the bowl. By then, the sport had changed drastically, but without a bowl team, the coach was a failure. And Leahy would have brought them a bowl team. Or so the reasoning went.

Perhaps that is moving ahead too swiftly. This is the story about the bowl teams that made Frank Leahy great and took him to Notre Dame. The name of the game was football and to Leahy, football was win, win, win . . . and his players had better be in shape to win it.

And they were.

Run, jump, fight, push, shove, get the yardage. Never forget your assignment. Meantime, keep high enough marks to retain your scholarship. And go to church on Holy Days.

That's what is called a full schedule.

My sophomore year brought the Sugar Bowl. It was also the year of the Georgetown game. Some still say that it was the greatest college football game ever played.

Grantland Rice wrote, "On this beautiful sunlit afternoon in Boston I have just witnessed, after covering 40 years of football, the most thrilling game of my career."

I scored a touchdown in that game. Not much, really. But we were playing both ways in those days.

We stopped Georgetown on their final series and with 28 seconds remaining had a fourth down situation near our own goal, leading 19-16.

This was where the Leahy style of coaching came in. Leahy's first gesture to a new player was presenting him with the rule book. If the player didn't know the rules intimately, then he didn't play for Leahy.

Henry Tosczylowski called the B.C. plays. We gathered in the huddle, broke, and the ball was snapped.

I looked backwards and Charlie O'Rourke was running around in the end zone, up and down, back and forth between the goal posts. Georgetown was stunned for a couple of seconds, then they started in after him. We blocked and shoved and the gun went off.

An intentional safety.

We won, 19-18.

The Leahy rules. Always something that can be done. Later, there was much talk that the play had been sent in from the bench. Possibly. I will never know. I can't remember anyone coming up with the play. Indeed, I still know my first thought when I saw O'Rourke running around back there—"Holovak, you've missed a block. They've chased him in."

That made us the national champions again and after beat-

Frank Leahy

Boston Record American—Sunday Advertiser

The Sugar Bowl team

Holovak (arrow) plunges through Tennessee line for touchdown from one-foot mark in the Sugar Bowl game

Boston Record American—Sunday Advertiser

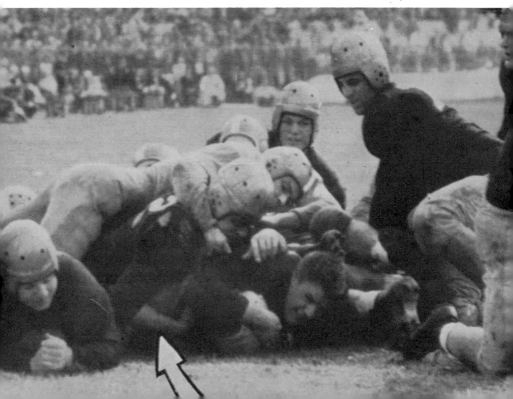

Boston Record American—Sunday Advertiser

Charlie O'Rourke (13) runs 24 yards for final touchdown at Sugar Bowl, with Holovak blocking

ing Holy Cross we were off to the Sugar Bowl. Leahy minced no words. John Gillooly recalls his warning, "I want every one of you lads in perfect shape. I'm a very good friend of Mayor Tobin and I want you all to know one thing. If any of you lads get liquored up in New Orleans, then I personally am going to have the Mayor arrest you for being inebriates when you get home."

Fight talk.

The Sugar Bowl game with Tennessee was one of those fantastic things that could only happen to a team which had a Leahy for a coach and an O'Rourke for a single wing scatback. Here we came down to the end of it. I had scored once—

a Pennsylvania "Hunky" touchdown, head down and a cloud of dust from the 1-yard line.

The score was tied. Time was running out. Here came O'Rourke, the passer. There went the ball. But Charlie was going to run. "Toz" and I put out the block. Charlie was gone—24 yards. The ball game. The national championship. When we returned to Boston there were 50,000 people waiting for us at South Station.

Two important things happened in this game. Neither occurred on the field. Both made an impression for the rest of my life.

One was Civil Rights. I prefer the term Human Rights.

The other was a crap game.

Divergent? Certainly.

Anything can happen on a Leahy team. Remember that 0-0 time between Notre Dame and Army in 1946?

Human Rights came from a bad situation with a fine man. Lou Montgomery. An American. A Negro. Later in my life, I developed a philosophy.

I came by it hard. The best test in anything is learning. It may seem strange to think that I am a philosopher when I can't even be philosophic about a loss or a tie in a mere football game. Certainly, I don't want to pretend to be what I am not. But I do think that in a world such as we inhabit there comes with growth a certain knowledge, certain beliefs. When a man has these he should never back down from them. And when a man has experienced much, then he has also come to know the sheer priceless value of meeting every person and every event with a common understanding that each of us in his own way must do his best to accomplish what is right. March, I guess, to the distant tune of his own drum.

The point I'm making is this. Men come and go. As men. Negroes come and go. As men. Everybody is proud of his heritage. The American man who is also by accident of birth a Negro, and should be proud of being a Negro, was victimized by a lot of stupid people who ground him into the dirt.

And this was wrong. One thing that any grown Negro should do is be terribly proud, just as any Pole, Irish, Italian, or Jew should be proud, of his own ethnic background.

When the Czechs were all sent to the coal mines—or so it seemed—and got out, or the Irish came to Boston where the signs said "No Irish need apply," yet overcame it, or when the Jews fought their way out of ghettos to become leading figures in America, or the Italians grew to be great, so should the Negroes work to overcome the prejudice against them.

I was part of a team which put a Negro down. Lou Montgomery.

There can never be an excuse for it.

In my earlier years I tried to say it was because I didn't understand. I was just a big dumb fullback, just minding my manners and doing what I was told.

When the Sugar Bowl offer came to B.C. we took it. We went to Bay St. Louis, Mississippi, to practice. We came to New Orleans the day of the game. Lou Montgomery came. But he couldn't live with us. And he couldn't play. Because he was a Negro. This was in 1941. January 1. A whole world was going to war. And we quit on a big battle. We—as players —should have refused to play.

Lou went on to become a great man in his own way. Maybe we all learned a lesson. I did. As the years went on I learned it more and more. Never quit on anything. In football I've watched the Negro athlete—particularly, of course, the great, fantastically great, Jim Nance and the fine, dedicated Rommie Loudd—achieve significant heights.

The lesson here? Maybe pride. Maybe a man should be proud to be what he is. Maybe a man should be proud to be a Negro. Because they are undoubtedly a talented ethnic group to have achieved what they have with all the bad calls they have had against them.

On the train home, we saw a different example of bad calls.

Sportswriters are often a strong part of a team. Some of the boys got in a crap game in the men's room with some sharpshooters. They lost their bankrolls. Later, as the train moved north into the night, someone told Arthur Siegal, then the sports editor of a Boston newspaper. "Izzy" was always one of us. About midnight, he came bleary-eyed out of the men's room where the dice had been rolling and walked from car to car paying off the players who had lost money. Behind him came a porter carrying bottles of champagne. Our friend "Izzy" was the hero of the hour. The true national champion. But poor "Izzy" couldn't resist going back to the crap game one more time. In the morning, we bought him breakfast and gave him cab fare home.

Well, anyway, that's what happened at the Sugar Bowl. We beat Tennessee. We lost something, too.

Leahy.

Leahy was from Notre Dame.

They say it is a fever.

Maybe. I never knew Rockne. Regardless of what my Patriots' players say it was before my time.

Notre Dame. Where the statue of Moses has that finger up and the students say that means the Irish are number one. Notre Dame of the legends; of Rockne, George Gipp and the Four Horsemen. Notre Dame—where there had been so much football that the locker room pep talks came easy.

I can't give pep talks, but coaches have been making a living with such stunts ever since Rockne. They say Leahy made it at B.C. and Notre Dame that way. I don't know. I can never remember him saying a thing. Some of my teammates tell stories. Frank, I hate to tell you, but I have news for you. I never heard a word of it. Maybe that's what comes from being a fullback.

Anyone who ever played for Leahy has plenty of stories. They all run about the same.

Lujack's favorite story was about how tough Leahy was. Joe Signiago's nose was broken in a practice game with Northwestern and he didn't show for the Monday practice. Leahy sent down to the dorm for him and Signiago showed up with his face all bandaged.

"So why are you late for practice?" Leahy asked. "After all, what else can happen to a lineman except a broken nose?"

I do remember that in his second year at B.C. Leahy fell into a despondency typical of many big league coaches. I always view midgets as giants myself and people never really understand when I worry in advance.

Despondent before a game, Leahy could find any reason for making things worse. Once the father of one of our basketball coaches died. We were sitting in Frank's room the night before a game. Leahy looked up and said, "Well, at least he won't know the disgrace of seeing B.C. humiliated tomorrow."

The next day a man missed a block. A player on the bench yelled that he was a lazy so-and-so and a such-and-such. Leahy turned to the bench and chewed the yeller out, up one side and down the other. He wouldn't stand for profanity on his bench. On the next play the guy missed the block again. Leahy turned to the yeller on the bench and said, "I apologize. He is a ———— at that."

Two days later we had the game movies. Leahy ran the play over and over again. One missed block. Then the next. One missed block. Now he put the lights on. No one made a move. Leahy looked at the kid and said, "I am now going to run that film one more time. If you still miss the block turn in your uniform."

Then there's the famous story about the Notre Dame-Army game of 1943. For the national title. Notre Dame was losing 6-0 at the half. Leahy said, "Losing to Army would be like getting a letter from my wife saying my son had died. Lads, you know how I love that boy." It really fired up the squad.

But, someone else said, "Ah, Leahy was always cutting off an arm or a leg to win a game. He finally had to pick on the kid because he just didn't have anything else to cut off. He was a basket case."

I really think Leahy liked his players. That was just his way. Tough and hard-nosed and locker room orations.

Oh, well. That was Frank Leahy. He ran it like a drill sergeant. And he won. He would promise a suit of clothes to any center who could make the quarterback's hand bleed on the snap from center. He would be very rough on conditioning and body contact. Once he had a big tackle blocking. The tackle flattened the man, but Leahy was unhappy.

The man lay on the ground and Leahy called the squad around. "Lads, look at this man. Hardly touched. Hardly blocked. He wasn't even knocked down with basic tactics. Poor blocking. Poor tactics. Now I want this stopped. To win you must put the man down to stay. You must hit, hit, hit. Hit hard. Hit hard. I won't stand for anymore of this gentle play."

Leahy waved at the boy on the ground. "Okay, lad. Get up."

The kid stayed down. His leg was broken. Oh, well, that's Leahy. Or did I say that before?

Leahy went to Notre Dame. His contract was still running at Boston College. Indeed, he had just signed a new one. But, as someone said, he felt the call of his alma mater.

It is an interesting insight into the coaching profession. Any head coach would move to a better job. This was the chance for Leahy to really secure his reputation and the system is such that any school should always free a man who can better himself. When a coach enters this profession he knows instinctively that he will one day be fired. He must make the right moves at the right time.

This was the time for Leahy's moves. He made it swiftly and he was the greatest at Notre Dame since Rockne. The "psyche" part of it? Well, in sports they make a lot of the "psyche."

I may practice a little of it myself. But last week, the Boston Patriots beat Buffalo, 14-3. Buffalo spent a week looking at a blowup of a check which read simply, "$25,000," the sum to the winners in the Super Bowl. If that "psyche" didn't win, then spare me from all others.

Leahy went to Notre Dame and it started the Leahy image.

And we went down the drain. Excuse me. Not quite. Denny Myers—a very fine man—came into town. He coached us to a 7-3 record, which was good, but not a bowl team. The fans were on him. Two bowls in a row—Cotton and Sugar—and now we were unwanted.

Maybe it was a building year. Poor old Denny was later ridden out of town, but he had a lot of class. He never faulted us. We went along and went along laughing. It was before the war and it was a great time to be alive.

Great.

Perfect.

I have often heard about alumni taking care of players. I think it happens. I'd be a fool to think it didn't. This was 1941 and 1942 and I would now like to pay belated public thanks to some fine people who "paid me off."

First, there was Mario Gianelli, who later played so much and so well with the Philadelphia Eagles. My greatest failure is cards. Show me a deck and I'll show you a game. In those days it was cribbage. Thank you, "Yo-Yo," for all the nickels and dimes you contributed.

Then there was Jim Dealey. He was a candy salesman. He loved B.C. football. And cribbage. So he played cribbage. When he lost we ate candy and got fat. He also had a car. With a rumble seat. No player at B.C. that final season was more in his debt that I was. Jim always loaned it to me.

In fact, in that final season, I met my wife at a dance at the old Vendome Hotel after a game. Jim loaned-lost me his car in a cribbage game and "Yo-Yo" and I went to the dance. I only remember two things. The beautiful girl across the room and saying, "Hey, 'Yo,' you don't mind walking home, do you?"

"Yo-Yo" has never let me forget the walk home. Edith has never let me forget the dance. I've never forgotten how she looked that night.

This was a great time and a great town to be alive in. I must always say one thing—thank you to B.C. for having me. Thank you to my friends for what they did for me.

Men like John Curley, who was the athletic director at B.C. And Frank Jones. Once, in midwinter, I was down in Frank's training room just kidding around with all the others. The season was over. I had holes in my shoes. I was lying on the table and Frank saw the cardboard. He never said a word. The next day John Curley had new shoes for me. I think of that sometimes when I hear about modern athletes who have Jaguars. I'll take the shoes anytime.

Or Bill Cashin. He told me to meet him at Filene's, took me up to the men's store and said, "Here, make him a suit." It was the first suit I ever had.

More on Denny Myers now. When Leahy left we were dumbfounded. He was, after all, the man who made us. And the school. Myers was basically unknown. In 1941 he made a big impression on us. He was calm, he was confident. He made no big statements. We played the schedule and were 7-3. Good enough in most leagues, but not good enough following Leahy—remember, now, B.C., even with Cavanaugh, only played in three bowl games. The first two were following the 1939 and 1940 seasons. Leahy years.

Under Myers that first season we lost to Tulane 21-7, Clemson 26-13 and Tennessee 14-7. We beat Holy Cross 14-13. It was a creditable record. But they—that is to say, the dissatisfied ones—were out to kill Denny. As a matter of fact, they succeeded. He took us to the Orange Bowl the next year, then went into the Navy. He came back after the war, but he was playing such new tigers as Oklahoma and Mississippi and by 1950 they had wiped him out.

I always thought he was misunderstood. Coaching is tough. Coaching with rules of an Independent against a tough schedule is murder. Denny Myers was murdered, long before his heart attack.

Think of that sometime, when you are rooting at a college football game. Think of it when you are yelling for a coach's blood. He was a nice, funny, good, basically wonderful man, this fellow Denny Myers, and he was betrayed by an old image and an old legend. And by modern day football.

Denny was great in 1942. He had us laughing. He had us winning. Of course the war was on. Like any other school we were playing the last real season before going out to the killing ground. We were seniors and most of us joined enlistment programs. I joined the Navy V7 program.

It was our last year and we played the tigers and won by big scores. We had one close game—North Carolina Preflight, whom we beat 7-6, which was like beating the best in pro football.

Denny was great in practice. We had a huge tackle, Rocco Canale, who now runs a restaurant in Watertown, New York, and was a fantastically good college and pro player. Rocco took the role of our fall guy that year.

I can remember Denny with cracks like, "Okay, two laps around Canale and that's the end of practice for today."

We tore the opposition up and were bound for the Orange Bowl. I was an all-American. I was left out, too—from the war. We all had half our minds on the war. Except we knew that there would be plenty of time and knew instinctively that this was why we must finish school. It's darn hard going back to school after a war.

I guess a man only knows that after he has gone to one.

Our last game was against Holy Cross. After the victory we were going to the Coconut Grove for a victory party.

Maybe we had our eye on the Orange Bowl. Maybe we had our eye on the Coconut Grove.

But not on football.

I had 12 as the number of my uniform. Freddie Naumetz had 55. The game program had us both on the cover as co-captains.

It is said to have been a famous game. It has been said by many people that it snowed during the game. Maybe. I don't remember. It was only 20-6 at the half and the dressing room was quiet, but we were not terribly alarmed. We had won nine tough games, some by runaway scores. We were a great team. We went out for the second half and Holy Cross ruined us. The final score was already on the cover of the program—55-12.

Myers had class. In the first half, we might have scored an extra touchdown. That would have made it 20-12. He was asked, "What would have happened if you made that score?"

"Well," Denny said, "the final score would have been 55-18."

It was the most significant victory in the history of Holy Cross, our arch rival.

It saved my life and my teammates' lives.

We did not die in the Coconut Grove fire.

The locker room was silent. There is no point in talking when you lose by that kind of score. The only saver was our bid to play Alabama in the Orange Bowl.

In this period, there were only four bowl games and tradition called for undefeated teams. Football being what it was then, it was possible to find about eight teams to compete.

We were actually bound for the Sugar Bowl again, but when we lost they pulled out. The Orange Bowl group stayed with us, but the whole thing had an aura of failure about it. That shows you something about pressure football. Here we were with only one loss and already we were second best.

But that's how bowl games go.

Our saver was the feeling of war . . . and the Coconut Grove. I had Jim Dealey's car. I picked up Gianelli. We didn't want to go to the party. Finally, I said, "Look, 'Yo,' I just don't want to go in there."

He agreed. We went out to a dance at the Heights and were still fidgeting. Mayor Maurice Tobin, who later was to become Secretary of Labor, invited us to the Parker House. That saved us.

At midnight, we were in the lines standing behind the firehoses, and the people in the Coconut Grove were dead, including the equipment manager of our team, Larry Kenney, who was there with his wife.

Ralph Dello Russo, who is the equipment manager of the Boston Patriots, was Larry's assistant. He, too, might have been there, but like the rest of us he saw no celebration in defeat. I never look at Ralph that I don't think of Larry and wonder—was he there to meet us?

And we didn't show up.

The burning people piled up in the doorway. We stood on the firelines. The strangest, saddest thing of all was what we saw as the firemen and the police took away the poor burned, horribly dead people.

On the street, washed wet by the fire hoses, was the cover of the Boston College-Holy Cross program—Holovak and Naumetz, 55-12.

3.

An Empty Bowl

EVEN THOUGH I was an All-American again, the Orange Bowl could never be compared to the important things.

The war was on.

Out there. Bulkley was riding PT boats around Subic Bay.

Bataan.

Wake.

Guam.

A Japanese task force was following up its Pearl Harbor raid by moving on to the South Pacific.

A madman in Germany was declaring war in a three hour speech.

Franklin Delano Roosevelt was sitting in a corner of the White House on December 7. Late afternoon. His son, James, a Captain in the Marines, came in and the President of the United States was working on his stamp album.

"It's bad, Jim," the President said. "It's bad."

And we went to war.

We felt like freaks. Our college had a date in the Orange Bowl. Our degrees were two months away. We were in the Navy but not yet part of it.

So we went to the Orange Bowl.

Alabama.

The first series I ran 65 yards. Touchdown.

For a long time it was a record.

I scored three touchdowns. It is still a record, I think. Or at least some of the yards gained and so forth are. Frankly, who cared?

No matter how many touchdowns I scored, the Orange Bowl wasn't a great game. We weren't winners and they pay off on that. It had its moments, though.

Canale was winded, staggering around. He didn't have a sub because Naumetz dropped the water can on "Yo-Yo's" toe just before the game.

An Alabama player said, "What's the matter fat boy, tired?"

Rocco could only look up and say, "I'm so tired I can't even punch you in the mouth."

We lost, 37-21. Later, some Alabama players said they knew we would lose. One told Gianelli, "We knew you would lose when we saw how much you were eating at the hotel. You guys were shoveling it in."

I offer an apology to the shade of Myers. Denny, we let you down. The only excuse I can make is we didn't think. It was another bowl team for B.C. The third and last of its history. But it was January 1, 1942—and the call was out.

Far out. I am a man like anyone who is afraid. I dream of always living a life of peace. But by the God who runs any man's destiny, the game was 11,000 miles away and the plays were at Mariveles and Mindanao and Brisbane and Port Arthur and Finchaven and Itapi.

I graduated in February. The next day the V7 program put me in Navy O.C.S. In three months I was a ninety-day blunder. In three months and ten days I was married and exactly what I wanted to be—a married ensign in PT boats.

I applied for PT boats. Probably because of Leahy and the instincts he created within us. I just couldn't imagine serving on a cruiser and letting someone else guide my destiny. The competitive urge, I guess. Anyway, they said that in the PT boats they let you make your own decisions.

They told no lies.

I was assigned to Melville, Rhode Island.

Some adventurers were there. Commander Bulkley proved PT boats in the Philippines. He finally took MacArthur out, then came home to teach us "blunders." Sometimes, he must have wished that the Japs had gotten him.

4.

The Old Pros

BY 1945, I guess we could all be called Old Pros. Most of us had been away.

There is no great point in discussing my Navy service except for a quick passage. It was the first team; I was on it. I have always felt very badly about war, particularly about the people you have to kill and the friends you see killed.

But if they are going to have a war, then I think everybody should want to be out there. It is like being on a squad. Naturally, you want to play.

Our playground was the southwest Pacific. After Jack Kennedy became President, it seemed that everyone served with him. Apparently, I'm the only one in PT boats who didn't. I never met him. He operated in the Marshalls. We operated in New Guinea, New Georgia and the Philippines.

First we were commissioned at Northwestern Midshipman School, got married—didn't every Naval Ensign celebrate that way?—and then went to war. Some took their boats out. Some went out to join squadrons. I was one of the latter. Bulkley's book gave us a name: *They Were Expendable*.

In truth, we never felt expendable. We enjoyed it. In later years I have served on aircraft carriers and destroyers and cruisers and I admire the men who do it. But nothing could beat the challenge, the satisfaction, the true knowledge of life, of being on your own boat with your own crew.

I had a lot to learn. My first skipper was Joe Ellicott with

Squadron 7. Old Joe lives in New York now and he must have put up with a lot with me.

He taught me and I learned, and as time went on we went out on a lot of patrols together. Just for an historical note, there were twelve boats in these squadrons. You patrolled every other day. The theory was to keep the Japanese from resupplying their lines. Considering the jungles, it was easier for them to move their supplies and troop reinforcements by barge along the coast. In daylight hours our aircraft patrolled the area. At noon on a given day, two boats from Squadron 7 would leave Itapi and begin their mission along the zone. As dusk fell we would be in position and all night long we could run along, one boat covering the other, feeling for barges or for shore batteries. The engagements were just like any other engagements.

Darkness. The boat running with the mufflers down. The sound of the birds and the animals in the jungle. Suddenly you see something, you push in the throttle and swing over your 20 millimeters, your 37 millimeter, your 40 millimeter, the 50-caliber machine guns and the rest of the armament, and engage.

Sometimes the barges have good protection from shore batteries or from their own gunboats and it gets violent and exciting and challenging.

Standing at the con in this little plywood boat with a fourteen man crew, your guts are up in your mouth as you run fearful, and the radar operator, crouched down in the little hole to the left, reports blips on his screen.

The moon is down on these nights and it is all darkness. And the white phosphorescent wake of the boats and the dull sound with the mufflers just burbling and the radio begins contact and the count down and the patrol commander says into the TBF, "Ready . . . execute." The boat goes into her turn and the mufflers come off and the boat is screaming down at thirty-five knots with the bow whacking into the waves and pounding, pounding, pounding, and then the tracers start arcing out like a long bomb touchdown pass and are finding and hitting and the 20 and the 40 and the 37 are firing those orange blobs—just like a football—long and up and down and wh-a-a-m, whoosh, w-ha-a-a-m, and the barges are being hit and the shore batteries are firing back at you and you make the first sweep and put the wheel over and come around and engage from the other side and it is done all over again and men are yelling and screaming and cheering, perhaps, who knows what they do at this moment? There are screams and the water breaks up and comes warm and wet over the con as a shell explodes; the boat shudders from a quick smash against her side and for a second your heart hesitates because she is hit and going down and then she digs her stern in and puts her bow up and slashes back again.

Suddenly, it is all over. There are orange-red-purple-pink flames and oil is spreading on the water behind you and the boat makes the last turn and disengages and in the after action report it will say that two barges, troops and cargo, were sunk at a grid point that will never be remembered again for any other purpose.

Behind, men are drowning or swimming to shore or sinking with their wounds bright red and bubbling and then there is the silence and only the jungle birds and only the echoes in your mind of the world of violence and the boat's rendezvous and turn for home.

The sun comes up and we watch for Japanese airplanes. One almost gets us. Another day, we get one, watching this brave man bring his flimsy little thing in and catching him in the crossfire of two boats and leading him and then seeing smoke, first a puff and then dark, black, dirty, and the Japanese fighter goes over on its back and staggers a little like a punch-drunk tackle and rolls out and then the nose comes down and he is gone into the sea. There is a splash and a long, low noise comes back and the boats keep going home toward Itapi. It will be one more small note in the after action report and behind us another man—a good man, maybe, a fine man, maybe, but the enemy—is sinking in what remains of his cockpit and today I sit writing a book and the man who might have had every right to kill me and write his own book is a bald skull in a rusty fuselage somewhere at the bottom of a deep lovely blue sea.

So that is the way it went. No better, no worse than anyone else's war. Home in the morning sun and back by noontime. A twenty-four run and then twenty-four hours—or, if you were lucky, forty-eight—to refit. Then out again. Sometimes the missions were more exciting.

Sometimes we took out Rangers on an intelligence drop behind the lines. There was no moon these nights. Two boats, twenty-eight men, and six Rangers with a rubber raft. Head to a given point, about 500 yards offshore, and if they liked the setup then they would drop the raft and wearing all that blackface would climb into it and be gone.

The boat would sit there, maintaining station, waiting for the little gleam of a flashlight. Flick . . . flick . . . flick and they would be coming out and we would cut the engines in and head toward the shore and pick them up, standing at the guns, ready to engage, grabbing the raft and the men and then heading out to rendezvous with the other boat. Then we would head home again.

Once they went in—these men we never knew, never heard of, never saw again—and picked off one little Japanese, who was the last man in a patrol. Hit him over the head, brought him back to the raft, flashed the light and paddled out towards us as we roared in. We made the pickup and headed home and the poor little Japanese woke up on PT-131, his whole world behind him.

A cameo scene. Just one I remember.

Holovak the ensign had a lot to learn and these were good people, these crews, who operated on a teamwork concept. The only time I ever failed to follow the rules of the team was in December of 1943. Everyone was taking atabrine to guard against malaria. But the atabrine turned the skin yellow. Stupidly, I didn't take the pills. On Christmas Eve, 1943, they carted me off to the hospital. For two weeks it was touch and go. But you can't kill a "Hunky"—especially not a fullback who played for Leahy and Myers.

Wally Lemm, even though he wore glasses, was skipper of PT-114 in Squadron 8 and invited me over to share his fun. I transferred as his exec. Wally's eyes went completely bad and the sent him home and I was the skipper. And that's about the way it went.

Squadron 8 went roving. We had some action and we had some quiet times. The boats were always sitting ducks for planes and we always went in pairs and there was always a rule about rendezvousing again for a pickup in case the other boat was hit. We were hit a few times, but we never sank. Sometimes when a boat would sink the crew would just go over the side and float and wait. God, it must have been a horrible experience. I'm glad I never had it.

The time finally came to go back home. Fifteen months and the tour was over and we went to Brisbane and got in the troopship and headed home. Along the way we met the "Papa Bear," George Halas, an old man even then, but no one was ever going to keep the "Papa Bear" out of war.

We talked. Football. But the "Papa Bear" was a commander. I wasn't going to spend much time around commanders with my rank. So I headed home to Melville for retraining and refitting and arrived back in Boston just in time to take Edith and my six-month old daughter Michele—she's twenty-two now, where did the years go?—Christmas shopping. And came down with malaria again. And went to Melville, Rhode Island.

We were supposed to have three months off, but if you had malaria they gave you three extra months. So we settled in Melville and football began again. Just another malarial jockstrap. Player-coach of the Melville, Rhode Island, PT boat school.

Behind me memories. Some good guys. Alfred Gwynn Vanderbilt was out and Torby McDonald, a lot of fine men. They went adventuring. They came home. I still hear from some of them as bouncing from town to town. Every April they have a meeting in New York and, darn it, every April I plan to go. But I never quite get to it. Perhaps it's football.

Perhaps it is just that case of—what did Thomas Wolfe write?—"You can't go home again."

It will probably be a disappointment to see them all now; fat, old, grey, remembering.

The only rememberances, I guess, are those that come from when they were young. That's the way I would rather remember them. Young and gallant and wild and courageous, misunderstanding, misunderstood, willing, afraid, unafraid, yellow under their tans from the atabrine, cockily wearing their shorts and their skippers' caps and taking those boats out from Itapi and Finchaven, two at a time, with the wake trailing behind them and the guns cocked and loaded and a night on patrol off New Britain ahead of them.

I'm glad I went. I think anybody would be. It was not good to have a war. It never is.

But it would have been a shame not to have been on the team.

5.

National Football League

MY EXPERIENCE as a coach began against Doc Blanchard and Glen Davis in 1945—the year before they played Leahy's Notre Dame team to a 0-0 tie in what was then billed as the game of the century. Ridiculous, of course. "Game of the century." We keep having these games every ten years or so.

I would like to say that we beat Army. We didn't. But we did score more points against them than anyone else. And we were leading at the quarter.

The game with Army was arranged because ranking colleges canceled them. Melville was 4-0, not bad, considering that we trained at the Officers' Club.

As player-coach, I was the key figure. Therefore, it fell always upon me to be sure that the team had plenty of time to get to the bar before it officially opened and became crowded.

I have never taken a drink in my life—of hard liquor, that is. An occasional beer. This was the period of the beer. Occasionally, I didn't have one. Like between noon and one P.M. The bar was too crowded then.

Not that I was a lush. I guess we were all just happy to be alive. We were scheduled to go out to the Pacific again, but the war ended and we were just marking time waiting to get out.

Riding the waves—or rather the suds—of this 4-0 record, we ran into Army.

At the quarter we were leading 13-0 and were definitely headed for the hospital. There wasn't a man left on the Melville squad who could breathe. These Army kids were wide open to being taken—indeed, I think we scored more than anyone else did and it was the first time they were ever behind—but they had an edge on us. They were in shape.

I tried to be cute and said to Earl Blaik, "Hey, why don't we just let the clock run? No time outs?"

He smiled. Army led 28-13 at the half.

I was still saying it when the score reached 53-13. Finally, they did agree and the fourth quarter—or the largest share of it—was played without stopping the clock. It was the longest fifteen minutes of my life, to that point. There was no doubt that each man on my team was about to die in the service of his country, or, at least, in the service of the Melville, Rhode Island, PT Boats Officers' Club. Glub. Glub. Drowned in the memories of old beers.

I haven't had more than one beer a week since.

These kids could really play the game. Blanchard was all sheer muscle and courage. Arnold Tucker was the same and when Davis went outside you might as well try to stop him with a gun, because he wasn't going to be caught.

Careers must have been a tough decision for these kids. They were at Army during the war and they all graduated too late to be in it. The pros would have paid them a fantastic sum. Some went, some stayed. I am particularly proud of this country when I think of a Doc Blanchard who sacrificed that money to become a jet fighter pilot in Korea and again in Viet Nam, and an Arnold Tucker who has been to two wars as an infantryman.

I saw a picture of them recently at a Football Hall of Fame dinner. With them were Bill Carpenter, the Lonesome End, and Pete Dawkins, the Heisman Trophy winner and Rhodes scholar. Carpenter later was an infantryman on two tours in Viet Nam and Dawkins wasn't so much of a scholar that he didn't volunteer to become a paratrooper and serve with the

Vietnamese Airborne Brigades. The medals were secondary to these men.

I believe it could be called class. In an era where some have little desire to serve, it is a proud thing to see men like these. Except, of course, if they are running up the middle and wiping you out as they did that day at Melville.

Fresh punk kids. Never even stopped to salute.

The war was over and it was time to play for the money. The National Football League was just coming alive in 1946 and the All American Conference was declaring itself in for a piece of the action.

I would like to say they fought over me. But they didn't. Some teams laid out a lot of money to men still in uniforms. I think it is no secret that some players were promised extra sums and were put on payrolls while still in uniform. It wasn't unusual for a man to receive two or three thousand dollars bonus and a pay check of $500 a month as a retainer until he was discharged from service.

The war was over. People were thinking ahead.

I'm sure that in this period some of the colleges were doing it as well. Remembering that Melville game, I recall one Army end, Barney Poole, who later went to a couple of colleges. After he had been playing college ball for nine years somone asked him the question, as he drove up to a pre-bowl game practice in a big convertible with his wife and kids, "Barney, why don't you become a pro?"

Barney's answer was simple, direct, and tells a lot. He said, "I can't afford it."

In my case, the Walsh boys came after me from Los Angeles. They didn't have to hurry. I might have been a 1942 all American, but I was now a 250-pound blubber. No one else was in a hurry to get me. I signed with the general manager, "Chile" Walsh, for something like $800. Edith and the baby and I went off to California to chase our fortune.

Seeking security, I requested and signed a three-year no-cut contract.

Two big mistakes. The first was the no-cut contract. It was wrong for me and I have never believed in it since—

although, in the latter stages of the A.F.L.-N.F.L. draft kidnappings and chicaneries I, too, participated in passing out such contracts.

The second was signing for three years. It guarantees salary, but it doesn't provide a chance to negotiate for something better after a good season. There wasn't much worry in my case. I wasn't having a great season. I was just another fat pro fullback, passing through.

This was the Ram's first season in Los Angeles. Actually, they were the first major sports team on the West Coast, so I would think that they deserve credit. At least the Rams explored the territory.

It was a problem year. Adam Walsh was the coach. "Chile" Walsh was the G.M. Bob Waterfield was the quarterback. Jane Russell was the mascot. Well, we had something going for us, anyway.

The Rams had come a long way. From Cleveland to be exact. They beat Detroit for the title, 28-21, in 1945, but the crowds were still so bad that they moved on.

Waterfield had two names. "Old Stone Face" and "Buckets." The latter stemmed from the normal—for football anyway—association of Water. Waterfield became Waterbuckets. Waterbuckets became "Buckets."

The other name—"Stoneface"—was one you just didn't call him to his kisser.

These were the gypsy days of the National Football League. They would now resent it at the management level, but deep in their hearts they will agree. Pro football was then an awfully long way from replacing baseball.

Adam Walsh had been one of Rockne's Seven Mules. He was a mule when it came to salary, too, but he was the kind of man they needed to keep the league alive in those lean days. Don't forget, anyway you cut it, this was a league they formed on the fender of an automobile for $25 a franchise.

Walsh signed Waterfield for $7,500. He was a particular natural for L.A. because he was born there. He had married Jane Russell after high school, then took her with him when he went to The Infantry School at Fort Benning. Only later was the Howard Hughes movie *The Outlaw* released with the big build-up which made Jane a star.

Perhaps the nicest thing was—and is—that the Waterfields, Mr. and Mrs., never changed. I don't think they ever have. We didn't have a lot to do with them, certainly. A professional team doesn't have much real cameraderie off the field. Just a rule of the game. But when they were around together, they were nice people.

On the field, Waterfield, was a horror. Jekyll and Hyde. Just the way a quarterback should be. Miserable. He personally defeated the Lions in the 1945 championship game, despite three crushed ribs. In that game, he called a play for a halfback and the halfback wouldn't go for it. Waterfield wasted no time discussing the decision. He simply said, "Pull the huddle together"; moved one step inside and hit the halfback a solid right hand in the mouth.

This was the league I was entering. Even our present day wild men never saw anything like this, or how we played the game that year. Tommy Harmon was also on this team and also married to a movie star, Elyse Knox. They, too, were very fine people. Tommy was a fighter pilot and had parachuted into a jungle and walked out. I think some of his experiences affected him. He was willing to try and he was great. But, there was a piece missing, as there was for so many of us.

We had a difficult time getting adjusted. I know the no-cut contract didn't help. We didn't drive ourselves. We didn't make the complete adjustment from the war to pro football. A small, valuable piece had gone out of us.

We were back from the killing ground and some of us were bloody and still remembering. The game itself didn't seem that desperately important.

Much later, as coach of the Patriots, I told this to Joe Bellino, who won the Heisman Trophy at Navy and served four years—including some in Viet Nam. When Joe came home to football everyone expected him to be great once again. It didn't figure and it didn't happen. He stayed in shape, but four years were gone and I took him aside and told him not to push it.

Joe had a no-cut contract, too, just as I did in 1946. But I had a prior experience. It takes a long time to adjust. Joe Bellino hung in there. Next year, for all the scoffers, I think a lot of people are going to be surprised.

My own adjustment began one night wiping the dishes. The dismal season of second place was long since over. Edith and I were at the sink when the radio announced Holovak had been traded to the Chicago Bears.

I can't remember my exact feeling, but I think it was first numbness at being expendable to the Rams, and then complete and utter joy to have a new chance and to be playing with the "Papa Bear"—George Halas.

Halas had an influence on my life. Later, I'll tell you how I got Jim Nance from him—which might have cost the Bears a title, because can you imagine Jim Nance and Gayle Sayers running hip to hip? Look out, baby, the roof is going to fall in.

That night, "Papa Bear" Halas called. Nothing in my contract said the new team had to pay our expenses, but Halas operated differently. He told me I was fat and out of shape and I'd better come into camp ready to play the game. He said I would weigh 212.

There was no question that I would.

The "Papa Bear" had spoken.

Then he said he would pay to move my furniture and all my other expenses. Considering that George wasn't long removed from the old days of the Staley Starch Comets, it was a pretty classy thing to do.

But it was typical. Halas was then pro football. He still is in a lot of ways. Go back to all the great moments and he is present. Except when he went to war as a fifty-two-year-old sailor. Go back to all the dark moments and he's there too. Standing like a rock. And throwing rocks when he has to.

The Bears were the champions prewar and during the

head-to-head 1942–43 period before the league marked wartime.

This was back when sportswriters and fans often compared college teams to the pros. At B.C. in 1942—the same year the Bears beat the Skins 73-0—the popular game was to question whether the Bears could beat B.C.

Beat B.C.? Are you kidding me? Some of those guys on the Bears looked like Neanderthal men. The name Bears came from the bearskins they wore. And "no fairsies" if you didn't kill the bear barehanded.

Sid Luckman was the quarterback. George McAfee was a halfback. Bill Osmanski—who played against me at Holy Cross—was the fullback. I had one edge on Osmanski. He was in his final year of dentistry. It set him up to be beat out. A sad thing, really. Tough, I liked Osmanski very much. Later, I would coach against him. But this is the way the pros are. You hold your job or you don't—which is what I mean about never being taken out for an injury. You may never get back in. How many men have made their reputations replacing injured stars?

Halas took no excuses. Example: he told me to come in at 212. I came in at 214. He put a rubber shirt on me and made me run off two more pounds. Even if I died. He made me a football player again.

Halas never believed in locker room orations.

The team was professional and was supposed to play that way. Sometimes he would get carried away with himself. Completely. We were in Boston in 1947, playing the poor Yanks and gathered together for extra movies and plans.

The conversation:

Halas: "You lost to Green Bay, 29-20. Do you know that?"

Luckman: "Yes, George. What about tomorrow's game?"

Halas: "Never mind about the Yanks. What are you trying to do to me, Luckman? You tried a 7-A and they very nearly took your head off. What are you trying to do to me? Get killed? You want to die? You want to leave me without a quarterback? You looked like you were trying to stuff that football in your ear. In your ear? You hear me? Of course you can't. You have a football in your ear. That's very unbecoming, Mr. Luckman. You try playing from now on without the football in your ear. You are supposed to throw the football, Mr. Luckman. It's not for your ear. It's to throw. McAfee, what are you grinning at? Do you know that Smith chased you into the end zone? The great George McAfee. Do I pay you for that? The great George McAfee paid to run backwards? That will cost you fifty dollars next time. Do you think I pay you for the fun of it? Losing to Green Bay? To Green Bay? [Almost a scream now.] Holovak. You, Holovak, you. Do I pay you to run forward? Then why don't you run forward? You ran against that line like you were waiting to run backwards. Let me tell you about this game. The idea is to run forward. You are the fullback. You are supposed to carry the ball forward. Do not run backwards when you run into the line. Run forward. That is the game we are playing, Mr. Holovak. Run forward."

So it went. We never did get the game plan. But we got the idea. The only thing sacred with Halas was winning.

The Rams finished second in the Western Division in 1946. The Bears—"Monsters of the Midway" they were called —were perennial champions. Being traded to them was like joining the old Yankees. Naturally, there were problems. I was traded for Luckman's roommate, Dante Magnani. I don't think Sid was ever in love with me because of that, although it never showed.

This was in the frontier days of the pros. *High Noon.* Two-gun time. Crazy, the sense of being a member of a team and the innate knowledge that by the very nature of the sport every man's hand must be against you.

My roommate at B.C., Gianelli was with the Philadelphia Eagles. He was fighting against another ex-teammate of ours, also another roommate. Only one job was open. In an exhibition against the Eagles I was hit by Gianelli and thought my teeth would come out through my head. Money and a job were at stake. Pride. Never let up.

This was the time in the training camps when we talked about "The Night of the Turk."

Or "the man in the crepe soled shoes." "The night crawler."

There was considerably less horseplay than there is now. Events happened too rapidly and too drastically. We would sense when a man was going. The man could sense it too. The Turk would be abroad with his long knife—and, zip, a coach would appear and the man would be gone.

It was an underlying, unsaid thing. After playing against the Eagles in that exhibition, I went to dinner with Gianelli and our ex-roomie. All three of us knew "Roomie" was gone. We never mentioned it. He was the next day. His buddy, Gianelli, had his job. His buddy Holovak ran over him once too often. His career was finished.

It took all kinds to make that league. One player's first play was automatic. He stepped back and went for a field goal between the legs. Worked pretty good too. Until someone used his mouth for a goal post. That's the way it had to be. We policed ourselves. We knew the wild ones, the cheap shot artists, the scared ones. The scared ones could be run out. The wild ones could be contained. The dirty ones would have their hands, legs, noses broken—anything we could get a good hold on.

It had to be that way. Just chattering with "Yo-Yo" now as I write this book he summed it up, "There were guys out there who would break your jaw without a second look. The name of the game was get them first."

That's where the expression "clotheslining" came from. It means hanging a man out to dry and is best done against a runner or a receiver coming downfield with his head turned. Simply stick out a long arm, supported by 300 pounds, and the head goes backwards while the body is still trying to run frontwards.

A game of which it could charitably be said—played in hot blood.

Sometimes too hot. Men died.

A violent game.

One inner facet must be understood about professional football. It is played by men who somewhere inside themselves have the mechanism which can be triggered by the supreme delight of savage contact, men who enjoy teaching a rookie never to turn his back or let up when a play is going somewhere else, men who will cream a star and then dance with joy, men who will just do things violently because they can no longer repress them.

Halas was experimenting with the T when he signed Luckman. He had a choice between Sid and Davey O'Brien, who was considered a much better college player. But Davey was smaller. Halas wanted height and established the pattern for pro quarterbacks ever since—pick a man who can get the ball over the big ones charging in.

When they first explained the T to Luckman—who played single wing with Lou Little at Columbia—Sid said, "Gee, coach. Those halfbacks are going to get killed."

Halas answered, "That's all right, Sid. Just as fast as you kill them I'll send you a new one."

An interesting insight into the team I was joining. The name of the game was—and always will be with George Halas —win.

That's what Halas looked for on his teams. I am certain that none of us were ever known as the gentlemen of the sport, although I can honestly say that "Papa Bear" never taught one dirty play.

George just wasn't the kind of man who could play that way, rough though he was.

George came to win. He never settled for anything less— except in 1925 when they made the first major change in college football and instituted two balls, one to remain on the sidelines to be cleaned on alternate plays. George raised hell. The extra ball cost five dollars.

With all of this there naturally were teams who came after the Bears more intent on mayhem than on the ball game.

Luckman tells, which I know is true, of the coach who tried to get his team steamed up: "And now we'll go meet the big bad Bears and get the hell kicked out of us and then go home and get drunk." It didn't steam them up, but he was right. They went home and got drunk.

The Bears of this period were the T-formation. Halas and Luckman proved it would work. As a matter of fact, Luckman and Halas had a long session once with Leahy, who came to see how the T could be used in colleges. Both came away impressed—if exhausted. The meeting was in a restaurant and after eight hours Leahy was still working our formations using chairs. He went back to Notre Dame and threw out the Rockne box and modernized college football.

Playing for Luckman was a good deal for a fullback. He was a fantastically capable quarterback who allowed little room for emotion or error. The only time I ever remember Sid losing the game of one-upmanship was when we led by 44 points with a few minutes remaining. Sid turned to the linemen in the huddle and said, "Okay, we're on our 20. You guys are always complaining. You run the plays. We'll start with the left end and work across."

By the time Sid reached right tackle we had a touchdown. That was the last time Luckman made that mistake.

Halas had 350 plays. Each was designed for a touchdown.

Except for the years I played. Twice we were beaten for the division championship by the Chicago Cardinals.

The first time I blew it myself. And learned a good lesson.

A great team, the Bears—but losers. Three quarterbacks: Luckman, Johnny Lujack and Bobby Layne. Poor Layne never did get much of a chance. But he went on to prove out. Lujack never developed, because he had too many talents. People forget that he was a superb defensive back. Luckman was so competitive that we had to give him credit. Whatever else he was, he was a quarterback first.

The Cards were our poor relations. This was before Halas finally chased them to St. Louis. Two franchises in one town were more than George could bear. The poor Cardinals received little publicity and played mostly before friends and relatives. And most of their friends went to the Bears' games.

In 1947, Jimmy Conzelman coached the Cards. Paul

Christman was quarterback—the same Christman who now does such a fine job on N.B.C-TV with Curt Gowdy, a broadcasting team which I feel really puts you inside the true picture of football.

Christman was not above making up plays. Above it? He thrived on it. One thing with Christman—the advance movies wouldn't do you any good. We never knew what he would do next. If he survived to play in today's pro league, he would probably be a modern legend. Paul's a good old-fashioned one anyway.

He began his reputation in 1946 after he was discharged from the Navy. The final game against the Bears, who had the title almost clinched. In 80 seconds Christman threw three touchdown passes and tied the score 28-28. With 0:04 left, Conzelman was on the sidelines giving the sign to go for a field goal. The Cards were on the Bear's five.

Conzelman was jumping up and down as if he were in a can-can lineup and someone said to Christman, "I think he wants a field goal."

But the end, Mel Kutner, told Christman, "I can fake their half out of his underwear. Can you hit me?"

Christman said, "I can hit you."

Kutner said, "Well, tell Conzelman you understand." So Christman waved to the coach that he understood for the field goal and then stepped back and passed for the touchdown.

Christman was selected Quarterback of the Year. Conzelman fainted.

This led to a great line the next season. Someone asked Conzelman how the Cards would do. He answered, "How do I know? I'm only the coach."

Conzelman had his hands full. Against Green Bay, Christman came up with a beauty of a fancy Dan pass that didn't work. Conzelman wasn't angry. "The horrible thing would have been if it had worked," he explained.

Once Conzelman sent in a sub. He trotted back to the sidelines and said, "Christman doesn't want a sub, coach."

Conzelman patiently said, "Well, just go back out there and tell him you're not a sub. The ———— has been playing with only ten men for the past five downs."

Conzelman was far from stupid. He just had wild horses.

After they beat us, the Cards played the Eagles. Comiskey Park was frozen and the Cards decided to wear sneakers. The Eagles meanwhile were filing their spikes down.

A club house boy told Conzelman, but Jimmy refused to protest. Until the game started. Then every time the Cards needed 5 yards he had a player point to a pair of Eagles' shoes. 5 yards, illegal equipment. 35 times 5 would have been too much for Greasy Neale of Philadelphia to take. So he changed shoes.

Greasy was not above getting a little emotional, too. Charley Trippi—who often took the long way home—ran about 150 yards against the Eagles for a touchdown. One Eagle missed Trippi right in front of the bench. Greasy had the word for the moment. He looked down and said, "Get up, you lazy Bugger. He'll be back in a minute."

Well, these were the wild old days. It can't happen now. But it happened then. And happened to me. Coaching lesson: The last game of 1947—the big one—a sellout crowd and all we have to do is beat Christman and Conzelman and Kutner and we're the champs.

We kick off. They get the ball on their 20. In the huddle—as it turns out later—Christman looks up and sees Babe Dimancheff still there.

The Babe was only in to run back kickoffs. Conzelman forgot to send in a sub. Christman asked, "Hey, Babe? What are you doing here?"

"They didn't send out a sub."

"Okay," Christman said. "Tell you what. You're fast. Run down past Holovak and I'll throw you a pass. You can outrun him."

They came out and we immediately noticed that Dimancheff was the odd man. But Kutner was the pass receiver and when they came into my zone I had an option and moved over to help on Kutner. Dimancheff stepped on it, went right past me and Christman hit 80 yards worth of touchdown. For the rest of the game we chased, but could never catch up.

Felt low? Oh, back to gravedigging. I don't mind telling the story now, although I noticed in Murray Olderman's very fine study *The Pro Quarterback* that Christman diagrammed the play without mentioning the Bear whom the Cards embarrassed.

Well, it was me. I blew it. I learned two things. Always cover your zone. Never help out. Stay with the game plan, even if the numbers change. This is how I coach my team. So I guess I owe Christman a vote of thanks in a way. It was a hard lesson to learn, but it paid off with the Patriots.

The Cards beat us the next year as well. For the title. That was the season we went to two platoons. I was on defense. I loved playing linebacker. I guess the smothered emotion of violence or something. There is something about finding your man, reading the play right and then hitting him. I sincerely believe any good football player worth the name would want to be in on defense.

Losing to the Cards twice in a row for the title was something else. It could be summed up by something that Luckman said in the fourth period when a rookie quarterback replaced him. The string was running out for all of us old timers. Sid came to the bench after being whacked all over the place, slumped down, then in exaggerated fashion, looked up and said. "God. I'm grateful just to be alive."

So was I.

It was time to go. I never wanted to end my playing days sitting on a bench, milking another year just for the money. We see it often in the pros, but this doesn't make it right and it is probably the one true sorrow of the sport.

Denny Myers contacted me from Boston College and offered the freshman coaching job. The money wasn't much, but the chance was there. I was caught betwixt and between. Hugh Gallarneau, my very good friend and the great Bears' back who was all America at Stanford, had a job at Marshall Fields' and had one for me. Hugh wanted me to take it. But I wanted to remain in football, so I went to Halas. The "Papa Bear" wished me luck and I was on my way back to Boston College. Hugh later became vice president of the company, then went on to Hart, Shaffner and Marx. He's kidded me for years that I might have wound up a rich businessman.

Well-dressed anyway.

But I picked football.

I've never been sorry. Or well-dressed.

6.

The Leahy Mystique

ON DECEMBER 3, 1959, my old teammate, Gianelli, visited the athletic director of Boston College, Bill Flynn. "Yo" was worried that I would be fired.

There had been rumors for two years. I had just beaten the arch rival, Holy Cross, which gave me a 6-3 record against them over the nine years of head coaching. My overall record was 49-29-3 and this included games against Army, Navy and some other rated tigers.

I was New England Coach of the Year a few seasons earlier. And I had never had a losing season after the first one.

Votes of confidence resounded all over the place. Bad sign. Flynn assured "Yo-yo" that there was nothing to worry about. That was noontime. At 12:15 Flynn came into my office and said, "Mike, the decision is not to renew your contract."

No hard feelings were involved. I had known for two years that Boston College was going to "give it to Mike." That was the old cheer they had for me in the great days of the bowl teams. It figured that some of the more hostile alumni would use it as their rallying cry again.

I sat in the office all morning, waiting for the door to open. My contract was up the next day, December 4. I was just sitting there, dreaming. My biggest dream had been to revive the old Leahy days, to bring a bowl team to Boston College again. But, I was running against the Leahy mystique. I didn't have the bowl teams and the old, rabid fans wanted another Leahy—or wanted *the* Leahy—and the wild, soaring old days of victory. I couldn't even get mad about it. Some friends said I should be prepared to make statements. I didn't feel that way.

Perhaps it was pride. Perhaps it was just understanding the game. I gave my best and the dream didn't work and it was time to pack it in and move on. Hard, cold, but time. Time to do the thing all coaches must do—accept being fired and then announce publicly that I had resigned.

I knew it would happen when I signed. Every coach knows that finally he will sit all alone in the office, with the unpaid bills, and wait for the axe to hit him in the neck.

Give it to Mike.

The lonely time. It's remarkable how friends and cheering alumni will forget. But it's nothing to get upset about. A rule of the game.

Really, it is more difficult for the families. When "they" give it to you—or when you have a losing season—there are many extra pressures on your family.

You win the first two games of a season big—but you know deep inside that the next one is murder—and you get murdered. So, the phone rings at home and someone asks Edith, "Was Mike at the game? Did he know what the score was?"

Some eighteen-year-old sophomore with pimples who couldn't make a good soccer team is all you have for a halfback, so he gets hit hard and fumbles. If the team is on a losing streak then the alumni ask, "How could he do anything else with such lousy coaching?"

We have won five straight and the fullback is an all America flop-out at studies. He can't play anymore. You execute the option—say he's hurt rather than embarrass him. The losing streak begins. They start yelling for your head.

A favorite alumni stratagem is to name a choice of new coaches. Once it was speculated that one of two local high school coaches would get my job. My daughter came home mad. I told her not to be so upset. "Why shouldn't I be?" she asked. "Isn't my high school coach good enough?"

A dream world. Soft green trees and quiet walks and the chapel bells and the smoky hush of autumn. The last practice before the first game. Worry. Fret. Fear. Gnawing. Tomorrow I'll lose 100-0. Nothing can save me.

The next afternoon we win, 14-13. A freak. But the alumni have the taste of it now and we're headed for a bowl at the Monday morning quarterbacks' club. Two weeks later, my daughter's high school coach is a genius.

So it goes.

Stories. The late-night stories coaches tell to each other. A guy wins ten, loses one, doesn't get a bowl bid. The proudest alumnus in town is the one who next day tells his gang, "I fixed him. I put a garden hose in his mail box slot and flooded his house."

Don't laugh. It happened. Or laugh unrestrainedly. It is funny, at that. If the coach can swim.

A coach is losing and his wife appears alone at a faculty party. The rumor is already round about trouble at home. Someone says to Mrs. Coach, "So Charlie isn't with you? Is it true he's interested in someone else?"

The smart wife answers, "Yes. He's always been interested in someone else. A fullback. A quarterback. A halfback."

But the rumors go on.

The mind always wrapped up in football, football, scholarships, scholarships. The coach goes to a luncheon with his wife. Later he drives to the practice field.

Thinking, thinking, thinking. The juggling act. "I'll move this kid in to plug up at tackle. I'll move the halfback to fullback." Thinking. Thinking.

"Oh, my God. Where's my wife?" The car drives back. She's standing in front of the hotel. "Well," she says, "I won't give you the touchdown, but you get credit for the extra point for coming back."

Then there are the wives who don't possess that kind of patient humor. We won't go into that.

We'll just go along sitting there in the quiet room of the athletic department waiting for the door to open and someone to say, "Scram, Mike. Go get another head coaching job." Thinking. Worrying.

How tough it must be on my family. The long bad year of losses. The worry lines at home. The kids and the wife sitting at dinner and I come home from the first practice and they have to be reassured. "Will it be as bad this year? Will people yell at us and make fun of us all year? Should we plug up the mailbox slot?"

These are the kinds of thoughts I know they are thinking. So I try to carry them along. Ease them over it. Tell them little white lies while the deep knot of worry hangs in my stomach.

Me, I was lucky. They were mostly winning years. They were great learning years. Right up to sitting there waiting for the door to open. Right then I learned one thing. College coaches in this country make one mistake. They should have severance pay written in their contracts. Or pension rights. So we won't wind up sitting stiffed with no money and no paycheck coming in after tomorrow morning.

That's why I understand Bear Bryant and people like him. I don't think Bear makes any attempt to hide the huge salaries, the free house, the TV show, the other fringe benefits that go with his coaching jobs.

He coaches for colleges who want to make money out of football and add to their national reputation as well. In this day and age when we worry about what is happening to college athletics and ask if it is becoming too big time, I think the Bear could stand as an example of what is good in pressure football. And good *for* pressure football.

With the Bear, the college knows exactly what it is paying for. And gets good dollar value. I love some of the stories about him. Ed McKeever—Leahy's old B.C.-Notre Dame assistant, my first G.M. with the Pats, now my Chief Scout— tells some.

McKeever knew the Bear and Babe Parilli at Kentucky.

The Bear was often compared with Abe Lincoln. Finally, someone asked, "Coach Bryant, is it true you were born in a log cabin?"

The Bear smiled. "No," he said. "Lincoln was born in a log cabin. I was born in a manger."

I like even more the way he handles his own problems. When Joe Namath caused one, Bear threw him off the team for the season, even though it meant a bowl bid. Namath learned more manhood from that than anything else. To be kicked out of that Taj Mahal Bryant calls an athletic dormitory must be one of the most shocking things that can ever happen to an Alabama athlete.

It carries one step further. Later that year, Bryant was in New York for meetings. One of them was nominations for the Heisman Trophy.

The Heisman winner generally is a spectacular athlete. He can also be aided greatly by some good press clippings and that is why college athletic directors spend time building up players.

It was suggested that Bryant nominate Namath. "I can't, Bryant said. "He didn't play that well for me."

High pressure college football is just that. But there is a hidden class too.

There's pressure everywhere. Waiting for the door to open. Maybe I should have stuck to gravedigging . . . dum-de-dum-de-dum, drum you fingers. Waiting for the door to open.

I knew it would happen when I signed: Denny Myers was still head coach. I had the freshmen. It was a beautiful season, but the first days were horrible. September, 1949. I thought I would go stark raving mad. I missed the body contact. I missed suiting up and sweating and the wild camaraderie of the pros. I missed not doing it anymore. Not too unusual. Athletes from all sports who have played for a living tell me this is true. An addiction not easily lost.

But at least I was still with football. I was still in it. Myers picked the freshmen well and they went undefeated.

Denny was a funny man. Very funny. Very wise, very witty. Just a little too tender-hearted. 1949 was a bad year for him. 4-4-1. Probably the worst part of it was the game with Holy Cross.

Denny, remember, was the coach in 1942 when we were zipped 55-12. Now, in this—a lousy season—he got lucky against The Cross. The horses finally jelled on the final snowy day and when it was over, Boston College was 76, Holy Cross was 0.

Denny was lucky to escape with his life. They called him a butcher for racking it up, and talked of getting some assistant pro coach named Vince Lombardi as a replacement.

The next year he opened with a 7-7 tie with Wake Forest and closed with nine straight losses; dum-de-dum-de-dum, drumming his fingers on the desk waiting for the door to open.

Denny had class. There were a lot of candidates for the job. I was on his staff and I made no move for it. Denny himself put in a good mark for me. He called and told me, "Look, I knew the name of this game when I took it up. Take the job. I'm on my way anyhow."

So I did.

Great seasons. Boston College went about it properly. They still do. The team was an Independent, not confined by conference regulations, but confined by a desire to play it honest.

A full scholarship was the best we could ever offer and we managed to get some good boys.

A trite phrase, but true. Character building. A matter of decision for the school and for the alumni. If they want a good team with character, then you play it that way. If they want a great team of characters, then you play it that way— knowing fully that when you get some of these kids in the high pressure conference you are going to get some real beauties. They can't be anything else. They are professional athletes on the prowl among amateurs and some of them come to the freshman class in big convertibles with big wardrobes and big money. They don't receive the money straight out. No huge wads of cash. But more than enough to get by comfortably and, usually, their fathers are given a nice job somewhere, or perhaps a new house.

I don't agree with that approach. However, I refuse to fault it. The problem lies strictly with the schools and the alumni. They pay their money and take their choice. Sometimes they wind up beating their breasts and crying "cop" but it is they who are doing the robbing.

Football is football. Among the smaller schools, you'll find just as good football played with an old ball and a pump as you will among some big giants with all the trappings of a professional team. That is because they are playing in their own league. Under their own predesigned rules.

Money creates promoters. Some coaches travel under the guise of being just a devoted Little Boy Blue. They'll rob the school deaf, dumb and blind and then run to another. The schools aren't really that surprised. They knew the caliber of what they were hiring. It's only the alumni who become upset.

Don't fault the participants. To them, it is a livelihood. Some play it straight. Some grab what they can. Some just sit there like I did, drumming fingers, waiting for the door to open.

Some coaches have a flair for names and for psyching up players. They promote things like the "Chinese Bandits." It works. Because there are thirty-three players, three full teams. At another school you might have twenty-one. The coach plays it with what he has.

At B.C. we had some good, some fair, and some, period.

So we juggled. It made for a startling team. Some of their mistakes were so startling that even the coaches were surprised. Some of their good plays were the same way.

It was a beautiful game of football. Steady. Interesting. I would like to think we built character. Indeed, I truly think that we did. Some of them—with good educations behind them—went on to play in the pros, boys like my own Art Graham and Jim Whalen and Jimmy Colclough. Or the

N.F.L.'s Art Donovan, Art Spinney, Ernie Stautner and Jack Concannon.

It couldn't have been all that bad. The comforting thing was to know that when they did get out of football they would have a good enough education to go on to something else.

Or if they were hurt. they could still stay in school. It has been reported that it is not quite the same in some colleges. But those rules come as no surprise to their players. They know them before they sign their . . . er, scholarship.

Then came 1957. And Leahy.

There is no way to circumvent this story if I am to tell a truthful account of twenty-five years of football.

Leahy and I were friends for years. He taught me. In the service and with the pros, we often exchanged letters or calls and discussed football. When I came to B.C. we were temporarily out of contact. The years have long since faded now; the memories are less biting; and Leahy and I are still communicating, still sit down for long chats. The subject is still the same. Football.

That must be the one great theory Leahy gave to this sport: 100 percent attention and devotion to football.

Whether he used it or not, he always sought advice. If I ever learned anything from Frank it was that. I'll listen to anybody talking football.

He was also a great innovator. Once, at Notre Dame, he didn't have any tackles. So he inserted a double quarterback under center and a double wing with a direct pass and everyone thought it was great. The formation lasted just until Leahy found better tackles.

We tried some of that at B.C. It wasn't quite as bad as they say. We weren't always using halfbacks at tackle and fullbacks for guards and centers for quarterbacks. But we had limited resources and we made do.

The record wasn't that bad. In 1957 we were 7-2-0. I lost to Navy and Holy Cross. The first and the last. My days were numbered.

Billy Sullivan, the president of the Patriots, was involved

in the 1957 plot. I think he acted like a gentleman throughout it all. I not only don't fault him—I admire him for it. Because I don't think anyone has ever before known the full story.

At that time, Leahy was aching to get back to football. Boston College had a strong alumni which included men who dreamed of getting back to the great old days of the bowl teams. There was a logical association—Leahy and bowl games. National champions again. Wave the magic wand.

Billy Sullivan became involved because he and Leahy grew together. Sullivan was the B.C. publicist when Leahy arrived in 1939. Sullivan went with Leahy to Notre Dame. After Navy service, he left Frank to promote the old Boston Braves. Involved with that, incidentally, he received a letter one day from a little boy named "Jimmy" who was dying of cancer and wanted an autographed ball.

From that one letter developed a charity called "the Jimmy Fund" and today the Jimmy Fund Hospital is one of the leading hospitals which care for children with cancer and one of the finest research institutes seeking a cure.

I mention it because no one else will. Billy has always had the ability to do great things—Leahy, the Navy, the American Football League, the Jimmy Fund.

Anyway, after losing to Navy 46-6 and running out the string of seven wins, the word was out that Leahy would consider returning.

I never communicated with Leahy. In Denver, October 21, 1957, he was quoted: "I see no reason why anyone with as fine a coaching staff as they have at Boston College would want anyone else. Mike Holovak, who I used to coach, is doing a wonderful job. He's a fine coach and a real gentleman."

That was all I heard from Leahy.

Meanwhile, his friends tried to get him the job. They knew it. I knew it.

Just one of the hazards of coaching. It is a business like anything else. The sad part of it is that coaches can lose friends over it.

I felt sadder over that than anything else. The manipulations continued. For the next full season.

Dissolve into still another year after that. No one told me anything from their side. I certainly didn't tell them anything from mine. In matters of this sort, it is best to keep your own counsel and just wait it out. The in-fighting can be fierce. And always there is the team to coach.

I coached. 1958, 7-3 and a big win over Holy Cross to wind it up. The bowl dreamers kept working. 1959, 5-4. The last game was against Holy Cross in old, wooden Fitton Field.

I was walking along the fence with the team for the pre-game warmup. Sullivan was in Minneapolis for the first A.F.L. draft meeting, but he sent Pete Charlton to give me a message.

"Look Mike," he said. "As you know, we did everything we could to try to bring Leahy here in 1957. Nothing personal, but we've always been Leahy men. He wanted the job and we wanted to get him. But after 1957 we knew that Frank Leahy would never get the job.

"Billy got completely out of it. But we think it's too late for you. We think that the ground swell is so great that you won't have your option picked up. We're really very sorry. But this is a message from Billy—he has a new team coming in next year. The American Football League. He just wants you to know that win, lose or draw, you can have a job on that team for as long as you want."

That was it. I knew he was right. I just nodded and smiled—maybe just that silly foolish gravedigger's smile; maybe you get accustomed to fatalities, even an axe in your own neck, when you dig the six-by-sixes in Pennsylvania—and went off to coach the team.

I thought to myself, "Holovak, you're not too bright." When Vince Lombardi left the New York Giants to coach Green Bay in 1958, some Giants intermediaries offered me the job. I turned it down to honor my B.C. contract. Later, in 1959, another team offered me the backfield coach position. I turned it down, too. Now I was standing in front of the bench at Fitton Field and the wind was blowing cold and shrieking as it does late in the New England year and I was just a tired old nine-year veteran of college coaching with some clean white socks and an old pair of football shoes, trying to win for the old alma mater and wondering how you buy Christmas presents for your family when you don't have a job.

It was a pretty good game. We won, 14-0. Some of the press kindly gave me a vote of confidence. The B.C. athletic department said nice things about me.

I went home to Boston College. It was Monday morning and I was sitting there alone in the room waiting for the door to open.

Flynn walked in. When they axe you, the idea is to smile calmly. Go quietly. No blindfold, sir. Sorry, no cigarette either. I'm a coach. I don't smoke. Just shoot me down.

We agreed that the public statement would say that I had resigned.

So I was resigned to being resigned and I did resign and Flynn shook hands with me. The door closed. I was sitting there looking out the window.

Dum de dum.

"Yo-Yo" came rushing in. "I heard it on the radio. What happened?"

"Oh," I said, "you know, 'Yo' that's the way the Yo-Yo bounces."

A couple of other friends came in and we just sat there sort of throwing the bull. I was thinking I should be mad. I was just numb. Just sitting wondering how to tell Edith we were broke again, one check between us and back to gravedigging.

The phone rang. It was an All America high school player from the Midwest. The fullback that I needed. I talked to the kid and his parents for two years. I flew out to see him. I couldn't promise him a thing except an education and honest football. Everyone was after him. With Cadillacs and Lincolns. The kid said, "Mr. Holovak, I've thought it all over and I want to play for you and for Boston College."

I held the phone away from my ear for a moment and

looked at it. Then I laughed and asked, "Gee, Son, I'm sorry. But have you ever considered Holy Cross?"

I hung up the phone and picked up my old football shoes and walked out the door and into the American League.

7.

Coaching Lesson

IF WE ARE to go any further, then the next subject must be coaching.

Coaches have many styles. Some are flamboyant. Some are pedantic. Some are pessimists. Some are realists. Some are dreamers.

Me? I'm a realistic pessimistic pessimist.

From sad experience.

Three things a head coach should never do. Second guess any other head coach; hire friends as assistant coaches; become too friendly with his assistants.

Add to that a fourth—never trust an opposing head coach. Like him. Admire him. Be friendly with him if you must. But once you hit the field, never, never trust him.

In my college days I scheduled a game with a friend. I was not given much edge by the officials. Everyone said so at the time. They asked me to comment. I only smiled and chalked up one more coaching lesson—never schedule an old friend unless you have some choice of officials.

If there is any secret to being a coach—and I suppose all of us think we have our secrets—it rests in being like the captain of a ship. In the U.S. Navy, the captain of the vessel usually eats alone. It avoids problems when the captain must make decisions.

The same goes in pro football. I made mistakes as a college

head coach. One was in hiring my assistants. I had some fine
ones. I also had some very fine assistants who would have
been great if the head coach hadn't been still learning. The
result was I gave some of them too much leeway. I accepted
half-hearted work and tried to make it good and cheated my
assistants, my team and myself.

I never made that mistake again. My professional assistants
are carefully picked. They are experienced professionals who
have played the game at all levels.

They have a good spirit and a good relationship with me.
They also have some wild arguments, among themselves and
with me.

This is precisely the way I like it. When the argument is
over the final decision is made.

No hard feelings.

But I must be hard-nosed. If I ever chew them out, then I
want to be able to do it without any emotion other than that
of a head coach demanding proper work from an assistant.

It cannot be done if the coach is too close to the man. The
fine line must be drawn. It is the same on every professional
team. There is a camaraderie, certainly. There are meals
shared and airplanes and hotel lobbies to sit in. There are the
long hours of watching the films. There are the practice sessions and the game plan.

There is also that one moment before I take the field and
the three hours on the field when the buck stops right here. I
never pass blame down publicly. Privately, I have been
known to forget that I never lose my temper.

Some coaches go by teams. That is to say, if a head coach is
fired or hired away he takes his assistants. I do not have a
team. I would happily recommend anyone of my coaches—
and do it honestly, depending on the type of job which was
open. They are completely free agents. If I am fired—and
from the B.C. days you can observe that this is the practical
certainty from the day we begin—I would most certainly
want to place them.

But I travel alone.

My coaches are Chuck Weber, defense; Art Spinney, offensive line; Jesse Richardson, defensive line—which is to say, the huge four who slug it out up front—and Rommie Loudd, defensive linebackers. Weber, in addition to all his other duties, is the overall defensive coach. He has always been paid extra because he takes the bad raps when the defense doesn't work. Not publicly. But he can sure get an earful privately.

There is one job I have never filled. Backfield coach. I do it myself, because I hope that one day Babe Parilli will accept it. This may come as a surprise to Parilli. The job is there. I think he will make a great head coach someday. In the meantime, he must start learning again. The backfield is his natural place—and I laugh to think of the day when he sweats it out with a quarterback over the game plan and thinks some of the same thoughts I have had about him.

The reason I have never hired a backfield coach is very simple. If I did, I would have to fire him the day Parilli retires as quarterback—if I am still coaching in Boston.

The coaches, then, are the nucleus. From here it stretches out over a wide panorama—scouts, players, personnel, tickets, airline schedules, meetings, the draft.

Twelve months a year. Lombardi says when he thinks he is going mad in Green Bay he flies to New York, takes a hotel room, opens the windows and listens to the traffic. It reminds him of when he was an East Side kid. He feels safe and sane again.

I go out for a walk. Same idea. Or paint around the house.

There is no point in a vacation. Head coaches never vacation. We all have the same occupational ailment. A week, two weeks away from the action and we don't have enough to occupy our minds and come home vowing never, never to take a vacation again. This often makes for an unhappy wife. I don't blame her. Football is a mistress of sorts—an iron mistress of iron will—and when we become involved we're stuck with it for life.

Some head coaches quit or go back to being assistants. Maybe the smart ones. The innermost secret all head coaches must share is simple, stark and very direct:

"Someday it will kill me. Someday I will strain this heart once too often and I will fall over dead."

Very naturally, we all know each other. Some of us are ex-teammates or have worked on the same staffs. In one specific case which comes close to home, Wally Lemm of the Houston Oilers was an usher at my wedding, skippered my PT boat and named a son after me.

Wally has beaten me. I have beaten him. Once—in 1962—I hounded him right to the wire for the title, but he never lost a game and I blew it by half a game in the standings. This year, I ruined him.

There can be no pity in coaching. There are no ground rules. There are no unspoken sentiments. The idea is to go as hard as you can. I have had a part in causing at least three opposing coaches to be fired, one of them this year—my old N.F.L.-mate, Mac Speedie—at Denver. I never let up. The best game the Patriots played all year, offensively, was against Lemm in Houston. We racked him up. I saw him afterwards. He was stunned. I shook hands and said, "See you in the winter, Wally."

There is no communication when things like this are going on.

Only winter is for friendship. For example, the game at Houston. I was in the hotel. I never called Wally. Or vice versa. In some sports, you hear of coaches or star athletes of opposing teams who eat together or visit. In pro football we can't take the chance. A stray word, an impulsive statement may tip off the game plan.

Also, never knock the other guy's game. Who knows what troubles he might have? For example, Michigan State versus Notre Dame this year. There are those who ask whether Ara Parseghian should have played for the tie. I have no comment. Only Ara knew what Notre Dame was capable of.

Or the coaches who move around. Lou Saban went from Boston to Buffalo, won two titles and left to coach at Maryland. He said he wanted the peace of college football. As this season ended, he signed a ten year, $500,000 contract with the Denver Broncos.

Knock it? Not me. Coaches know. It's a tough business.

We just stay at it and learn and try to get better. Naturally enough, there are opportunists in this business as well as any other. There are liars, cheats, con men, hard guys, phony guys, good guys. We can't all wear white hats. Heck, I have a black hat in the closet, too.

Black hats—this year in Kansas City. The mysterious case of the kid photographer without film. It turned out that this young man once worked for an educational TV station and was given a sideline pass to all games. Toting his camera, he would stand beside the visiting coach and his quarterback and appear to be taking shots while they were talking. The team benches were side by side.

Then the kid would suddenly run down to the K.C. bench and talk to Hank Stram or an assistant. He was also the only member of the press allowed in the K.C. locker room at the half.

Sometimes what he told Stram or his assistant would result in a yell and a change of defensive plans. On two occasions there were interceptions. Against Miami there were six. Since we tied a ball game we should have won, you might think there was some business being done. Apparently the Topeka, Kansas, paper did. They suspected something earlier in the year and tracked the inquiring photographer for two games, Miami and Boston.

The emphasis was on the sheer coincidence of it all and it let the reader to believe there was skullduggery afoot.

I may be stupid—but I don't believe it.

If I did, I'd settle with Stram my own way. This kind of espionage just wouldn't work that well in the pros. If the kid was listening to me talk to Parilli he probably wasn't hearing much, because we seldom say anything. Except once in awhile, "For gosh sakes, Babe, what happened?" or "Mike, did you see that silly fink turn right when he was supposed to turn left?" (Of course I saw it. Just before the eyes popped right out of my head.)

The talking on offense is done from the spotter's booth upstairs through a set of headphones to the extra quarterback on the bench. If they have anything to tell me, I am informed by Weber or Huarte, or I get on the set. Weber has one phone to Richardson and Loudd on defense. The extra quarterback, Huarte, is connected to Spinney on offense. When Spinney gets mad we don't need the phones.

If they want to tell Parilli he uses the phones. Or Huarte tells him.

I will put that Kansas City story to rest in this fashion. It is possible that someone was spying. But it couldn't have worked. If they really wanted to know what we were going to do, they could have come to the public schoolboy stadium we use for practice and just sat in the stands and watched the practices all week. In the pros, you can't vary it that much once the game plan is set.

However, there is always the possibility of cheating.

It would be possible to eavesdrop on the coaches' room on Wednesday with electronic bugs when the game plan is given to the quarterback. Actually, that is all you really need to know.

Or you could just tie in on the other team's spotter phones. That will tell you just about everything.

I hope I am not too much of a do-gooder, too much of a Boy Scout, but I prefer to believe the sport isn't this way. I know there has been some chicanery in it—mainly in the battle between the N.F.L. and the A.F.L., and the N.F.L. and the old All America conference.

I know as well the stories of what some coaches have had to put up from owners who became overly excited. Or who bet. There were at least two owners in the old days of the N.F.L.—N.F.L., not A.F.L.—who were pretty well known to make serious wagers on their own teams. This carries sportsmanship just a little far, I think, even if you are betting on your team. Once a man bets money anything can happen—as witness one game where the team was a four point favorite with only seconds left and the score tied. They could have gone for the automatic field goal from close in, and won by three in the final seconds. Instinctively the quarterback moved the ball into field position at midfield. Now, a quick time out. Before the game, the owner told the coach and the quarterback that he had a tremendous sum of money going on the game and had given four points.

The scene: a hushed stadium. Rain falling. The quarterback trudges to the sideline to confer with the coach.

Coach: "What did you move the ball dead center for? What the heck are they going to think if we don't kick the field goal?"

Quarterback: "What shall I do? I'll go for the 83 pass, huh?"

Coach: "Okay . . . but if you blow it, for God's sake fumble on the field goal. I could never face him again if we win by three."

They scored the touchdown and were able to go home. Otherwise the owner might have left them in the other town.

But it is hard money. Another N.F.L. owner died in the middle of a game on which he allegedly placed a very heavy bet. Later, his team won. Reports told how a Nevada club paid the bet.

This leads to one other important subject—gambling. I may be a Boy Scout again, but I know the hazards of betting. I also know that it has occurred in the past—and not just as in the Hornung and Karras case where they bet on games other than their own.

In the furious old days, there were stories among the players about certain guys. Including this great one about the old quarterback who ran his team beautifully. Except one day when he took 10 points and was leading by 6 with only a minute and a half to play. Home free for about ten grand. The other team was held on their 40 in one last, desperate gamble. Now the quarterback had to come back on field for 1:21. It was essential that he both win the game and not break the point spread. He couldn't trust the runners—they're touchdown hungry and might break away. He very carefully threw three hitch passes for gains and moved down to the 21. Deliberate, careful, steady, a double winner in both the team's game and his own bet.

The last play. He faded back and threw into the end zone,

aiming it just high enough to miss the receiver. A beauty, on the line, but rising, not coming down. The receiver, who ordinarily couldn't go two feet off the ground, picked up an extra lift from the safetyman on a partial grab and block and hold and hoisted off the man's shoulder pads and made one of those picture catches, just tipping the ball off his hands and up in the air and then back down for a bobbling touchdown catch.

The fans went wild.

The quarterback was on his knees slamming his fists into the ground. They wrote reams about it and about the ferocity of the quarterback who never quit, who was so elated at victory.

Actually, he was slamming his fists yelling, "No . . . no . . . no."

Football. In the good old days.

There are always stories in sports. Baseball has a great untold one. It happened in Boston with the old Braves. The participants are still alive and they will recognize themselves, as will most ballplayers. I'm afraid they might also have good attorneys, so I won't tell you exactly who they are.

Anyway, the visiting pitcher was having breakfast in a good restaurant—this was before night baseball—and said to its owner, "I'll strike out so and so four times today."

The restaurateur bit. "I'll bet you $500 you can't."

"Done," said the pitcher. "Come out to the game."

He knew the batter's weak spot and three straight times he struck him out. Now it was the fourth and last at bat and he wasted no time. Strike one. He could see the money. Strike two. He could almost feel those five beauties. He reared back and threw the third one right at the soft spot. The batter just got a piece of it and pop fouled it up beside the screen.

The catcher—not in on the gag—raced back and was waiting for the ball to come down. This was a moment of instantaneous decision and the pitcher yelled, "Drop it . . . drop it . . ." but he could see that the catcher was going to get it, so he ran in and faked a helping hand and knocked the catcher out of the way. The foul dropped.

Then the pitcher went back and threw the third strike and won his five cees.

Stories. Harmless in a way. But true. Wherever there are humans you'll find betting action. I am sincerely convinced that as the sports have grown and as modern communications have opened up between both bookmakers (by phone) and the public (by television) that it is absolutely impossible to have a fix anymore.

This flies in the face of all the smart guys, the side-of-the-mouth wise guys who have to be in on the know. They will insist that when a quarterback has a bad day he is bagging it. Foolish.

There is no point in trying to be such an innocent that you pretend it never happened—or couldn't happen.

But it went out in the National Football League when Bert Bell became commissioner. Bell knew sports and Bell knew bookmakers and he faced up to the fact that where both were joined there would be action. So he instituted his own policy system and he conferred with the bookmakers as well. I know. I was in the N.F.L. then.

It must be understood that bookmakers are not gamblers. Now, they even look like accountants. Their whole operation is based on the 6-5 price which gets them automatic percentage if they balance the book. It includes a slight little nether world of raised and drop point spreads where they can win both ways if the books are properly balanced.

They have their own system of communication and they can immediately spot it if too much money shows up on any one game.

Once Bell knew that, he could spot the game and warn everyone extra sharply. And Bell always knew. The old days are gone forever.

Use common sense, and figure it out. The only one who could really bag a game would be a coach who gave an improper game plan (and even that wouldn't be sure, because you never know what athletes will do, anyway). Or, a quarterback. The national average indicates quarterbacks pull down $40,000 for a six month season. If smart guys are going to make a killing, they have to guarantee the quarter-back at least $200,000 for taking the risk of losing his reputation and his career. The minute the smart guys take a shot like that, they have to make it worthwhile with a bet of over a million dollars. When you make a bet like that—even spread around—it must show up for the accountants. Can't be done.

Besides, we have our own policing system. Every team has. At the beginning of the training season, the commissioner comes around and very clearly delineates what will happen to anyone even caught hanging around with suspicious characters. Anyone ever caught betting—and they would have to be—is guilty of a felony, punishable not only by expulsion from football, loss of reputation and salary, but also by a prison sentence.

We post a list of all bars, clubs and hangouts that are automatically out of bounds. We check the characters of people who may hang around with our athletes. We must realize one thing. An athlete is accustomed to being something of a celebrity. Some people get their kicks out of being close to him. The most natural thing in the world is to gravitate toward someone who fawns over you, picks up a tab or gets things wholesale.

Therefore, an athlete could conceivably meet someone undesirable. That's where our cop comes in. I know him. The president of our club knows him. I want no reports from him on the conduct of my players until such time as he is convinced they have done something wrong or are in bad company.

That is to say I do not believe in a spy system where every player's moves are marked down. My players are free men. The only time I want any reports on them from this detective is if they may accidentally have met and be moving into what could be a trouble area. Then it is essential that we all know and act fast.

None have, and I am pretty sure none ever will.

In 1961, I traded a very good player—and a very good friend of mine—for a foolish statement. Not publicly. I just let him go at the end of the year. It was the season we chased

Lemm and the Oilers. We played Oakland—a team which was a walking, screeching band of absolute ineptitude at that time—and beat them. Houston played San Diego and won. Now in the last game of the year, we were switching to San Diego while Houston came to Oakland.

My player was a very good man. He had one bad habit. He talked too much. He was very kind to the press, which is all to the good. However, there are certain times when you should shut up. We stayed for a few extra days of practice in Oakland before going down to San Diego. A writer asked him how we would do. He said, "I'm confident we can beat San Diego, but if Oakland ever beats Houston there should be an investigation."

That did it. We beat San Diego. Houston beat Oakland. My good friend the talker didn't play in the game at San Diego. Since the season was over it was easiest just to let him go.

But it's a long fall. And for a foolish reason.

Mark it down, anyway. In every sport—and I am sure this would even include the marathon—there have always been people who wanted an edge. The first problem is to recognize this. The second is to combat it and perfect the means of stopping it. It doesn't make the greatest reading in a sports book and I even hate to put these pages down in print. But it is an accepted fact of life and I can assure you that when the wise guys nod their heads and say "bag job" it is only because they are complete novices in the world of professional sports. We aren't that dumb.

In my profession, at least; it can't happen here.

Or—much better, to be very practical—it hasn't so far. We'll keep watching.

I mentioned bed checks back there. That is another problem of coaching. Here you are handling a team of forty relatively huge horses. Some of them are brilliant men who would do well in any field. Some are just giants with the emotions of a ten-year-old. Some fall in between.

Their game is violence and six months of their year is lived in hot blood. The most natural thing in the world is not to not to stick to the straight and narrow. At all times I avoid becoming involved in any situations which might lead to a knowledge of their sometimes strange ways of letting off steam. But if they are stupid that's different. I have only one penalty for stupidity. A trade. If I can, I trade the man down to a team which is more like slave labor than football.

You'd be surprised. Sometimes we can pick up a great player in our half of the trade. A guy tripped up and was hacked into a bad team. He learns his lesson and we never have trouble with him again. Stress *never*. He *never* wants to go back to the short money.

Players can be aggravating. Their stupidity. We train all week. We play fourteen regular season games a year. Their salaries average $18,000 and some get much more up to $60,000. On Friday, we leave on a road trip. Just because they're away from home, it seems like an automatic release.

By Saturday's practice I can take one look—I can take one smell—and tell who the playboys are.

I never tell them. I just dump them. It's easier that way. Go play for someone else. Those troubles I don't need.

But I never hold a bed check. My theory is simple. Pro football is the best way in the world to live. The money is big; the sport is great; the life is filled with all the sensations any man could ever ask. If they want to blow it that's their business.

Of course, this leads to another problem—the wives.

Bless 'em.

That last is called diplomacy. I know most of the wives. That's as far as it goes. I'm not anti-social, but I never want to be in a position of knowing any woman so well that I will feel badly about firing her husband.

Still they cause a lot of trouble. On road trips, too. Some wives must go. They fly commercially. We fly by charter. Here we are finally in a town for a game that counts in their pay check and their bankbook. And here they come trooping gaily into the lobby in their best dresses and hats, out to have a good time. Jolly, jolly.

There go my athletes. Not in bed early. Not thinking football and the violence game. Just taking Mama out to supper. Supper goes on until three o'clock the next morning. There we all are again the next day giving each other the red eye.

If there is a stupidity in sports, this really has to be it. Another lesson in the coaching book—Mama, stay home in the kitchen. This is business—not pleasure.

Thus far, it must seem that coaching is all loneliness and perhaps possessing much too big an ego. Being a stranger among your own kind. I don't believe it to be so, and I hope it is not.

I love football. I love the men who play it. But there must be ground rules. The players must know we will give them the best we can. We must know they will give it right back to us.

All coaches are different. As I take you into the locker room in succeeding chapters, I'll demonstrate that I don't work very emotionally. At least on the outside. Other coaches give the big spiels. Who knows which system is best? We just adjust, I guess, to the team. If I ever gave an impassioned speech, my players would think I had gone nuts. I expect one thing from them. They are professionals, not mercenaries. Professionals. I will support them. They must support me.

If they wish it, then I give them counsel. When I sign them to contracts, I give them what I think they earned, both being fair to the player and to my own bosses, the owners. In college, you pat a kid on the back. In the pros you put it in the pay check.

Being both a general manager and a coach has its problems. Many players don't like two hats. They feel if they argue over their salaries when the boss is wearing his general manager's hat, then the boss will take it out on them when he's coach.

This happened to Sid Gilman at San Diego during the famous or infamous episode when Ernie Ladd and Earl Faison were playing out their option in 1965.

The option is a part of the contract which protects both

the player and the team. As in any big business, it protects the team more than the player. Figures.

Anytime a man wants to leave, he can. When his contract is up. He notifies the team that he is going to play out the option—the one extra season—and if he makes that decision we can then trade him, or cut his salary by twenty-five percent and keep him for the year. Usually, we make an automatic trade.

I've never had that problem, but Sid did. Unfortunately, he also had dissension.

Ladd and Faison and three other players were invited to a pre-season press conference in San Diego. It was part of the annual tour of writers from all over the country. On the inbound flight they listed the players to whom they wished to speak. Ladd, Faison and Jacques MacKinnon were the choices and were brought in from training camp twenty-five miles away. Usually, the coach talks last, but Gilman wanted to get back to camp, so he talked and then left the room.

In response to questions, the players were putting the hammer on Sid pretty good. Including MacKinnon, who wasn't playing out his option. All of a sudden, the door opened and it became apparent that Coach Gilman had not gone back to camp. "I've had enough of this," he shouted. There was dead silence for a few seconds. All three players sat on the stage with their heads down. Finally, MacKinnon looked up and said in a weary, very quiet tone, "Anyone need a good tight end?"

After all of this happened, of course, owners in both leagues enforced a rule that if a man played out his option and signed with another team then the new team would be forced to give the original club a player of comparable talent. It ended some of the skullduggery that goes on. But the deals and the counter-deals and the con men and the moves will really always continue. That's part of the charm of sports.

Lesson learned: if you are a player about to knock the coach—make sure he's gone back to training camp.

Incidentally, no coach or general manager should be above

being rapped. That's why we have team captains. It is their job to carry complaints. A smart coach listens. He may only listen and say "no." But he does listen.

Another method of the players is the secret meeting. The team captains come to the coach and ask permission. This is prevalent in college. It happens often among professionals, as well. Remember, now, their whole world is football and a team. All the lessons they have learned since high school. Some outsiders might think secret meetings are ridiculous. This is the players' own way of policing themselves. Players aren't stool pigeons. They don't blow the whistle on a man not doing his job. Not to the coach. The money man. They will tell the player. Or, if they're unhappy with the coaching, they'll tell the captain. Why should a man earning $35,000 a year take a chance on coming to you and telling you to your face?

I'm fortunate. I don't think they have ever knocked my coaching. But I have always left the decision on team meetings entirely to the Patriot players.

As for the knocks. Well, I try to take them in stride. If I don't read the papers then I don't know I'm cut. Therefore, I don't bleed.

Interesting philosophy. Unfortunately, I read the papers.

Writers make me think of Red Auerbach, who coaches the Celtics—or did—and Auerbach makes me think of officals, which is another part of pro coaching.

Auerbach wrote a book which ridiculed writers so badly that I found myself thinking this was the Ted Williams story. Of writers I say—thanks. But you'll pardon me if I'm sometimes noncommittal.

Auerbach also admitted in his book that this yelling and screaming at officals was mostly an act, that fines the N.B.A. levied against him were paid by the team as an occupational hazard. In which event somebody was being misled for a number of years.

In our league, we don't publicly attack officials. Sure, they blow some. I'll tell you some cases in point later. We just have to go along on the theory that, even if they do blow one, they're trying. Everyone is human.

This doesn't mean that I don't yell at them once in a while. But there is a terrible hazard in putting into the mind of an official the thought of holding, or a personal foul. On the next play, it will invariably be fresh in his mind and he'll look for it and find it in your guy.

Most fines are real in pro football. Which is another reason I think of this as a big league sport. In baseball, big fines are assessed. Usually phony. Ted Williams was fined $5,000 by Tom Yawkey for making his famous gesture. But he never really paid it, according to Boston baseball writers.

The A.F.L. is a little too competitive. The rules are stiff. Enforced. Nobody loves anybody where money comes in.

This has an effect even on the owners. I have been fortunate with the Patriots. The owners—the men who put up the original sums of money, Billy Sullivan, Paul Sonnabend, Dan Marr, the rest—have never tried to tell me what to do. But they have died a thousand deaths sometimes.

Any team is faced with the basic problem of money. Money comes from fans. Fans only come to a winner. In 1965, the Patriots opened with five straight losses. Stories appeared in the newspapers that didn't exactly make me appear brilliant.

Babe Parilli was thirty-five years old and he wasn't doing a single thing right. I didn't have another quarterback and even if I did I wouldn't replace the Babe. When the best you have goes bad, you just stick your heart inside a stronger shell and hang in there and hope. Live or die with the best you have.

All the injuries—and the mumps, can you imagine mumps with grown men?—didn't matter. We were losing; we were not drawing at the gate; the solution was simple—it was the coach or the quarterback.

To the credit of my owners, they didn't panic. Sonny Werblin thought he had a smart deal going. He was stiffed with John Huarte's salary and he couldn't even play him. Werblin offered Sullivan Huarte's contract—for considerably less than $200,000. To Sullivan's credit, he never panicked. We talked it over.

Perhaps Parilli was gone. Perhaps Huarte could be a great quarterback some day. The question was—should we replace Parilli with Huarte now? The Jets had the $400,000 quarterback in Namath. We would at least be able to put new life at the gate with a $200,000 quarterback who had won the Heisman Trophy at Notre Dame and who was the Most Valuable Player in the College All Star Game.

I like Billy Sullivan.

I like being a head coach, too.

In my mind, I weighed the alternatives. I prepared myself to say, "Look, Billy, if you sell Parilli down the river then I quit, too."

But, I didn't have to. Sullivan said, "Mike, I know why you have to go with the Babe. And I know that the Babe may have several good years left after this. At the same time, I think that we should look ahead to another time. Let's suffer it out this year—forget the gate, forget the money—and after the season we'll pick up Huarte and we'll groom him for another day."

I walked away from that meeting with the lightest heart I have ever had in football. I knew then that I had owners who would always let me coach—and they probably never knew that I was within five minutes of losing a job I coveted like some men covet money.

Parilli didn't have the receivers that season. He didn't have the breaks. Maybe it was my fault. Then, all of a sudden, he started hitting and down the stretch we were winning. At the same time, we were dealing for Huarte for later on.

Billy arranged to give the Jets a fourth draft choice and one veteran player after the season. When the draft choices were announced in November, 1965, there was the notation that Boston was giving its fourth choice to New York.

The story got out. Beautiful. The last game of the year; my players were sitting in the locker room as if it were a tomb. New York wanted Art Graham, but I wasn't giving him up. I juggled my way along, trying to figure something out. I fi-

nally decided I'd give them a six year veteran, my flanker-
back, Jimmy Colclough.

There was a method in this. New York was up to its ears in
potentially good flanker backs.

I was hoping they might let Jimmy go on waivers and I
could pick him up again.

The last game of 1965 was filled with dread for all of the
players. Who would go? I called Jimmy at home that night
and told him he was it.

When the deal was announced, Jimmy was in New York at
the Jets luncheon sitting next to Jimmy Cannon. Colclough
said, "You know, I've been in this league six years and I
never got so much publicity in all my life."

Parilli had finished the season and was still my quarterback
and still somewhat secure. After all these years, the bad ones,
the psychiatrist years with Paul Brown, Babe deserved something. Especially because he could still play the game the way
it is meant to be played.

Huarte? He made my team and someday he may be a great
quarterback. He has to do it himself. He only started one
year at Notre Dame and he was a sensation and won the
Heisman award. Otto Graham didn't put him in until the
Green Bay-College All Stars game seemed lost then Huarte
became Most Valuable Player. It was said he rose to the occasion of competition.

I believe this to be so. But competition in the pros is every
second of every day. This is where you need the experience.
Huarte was robbed of that all the way along the line.

Colclough? The Jets let him go and I had him right back
with me again. He caught some more touchdown passes.

I dunno. Coaching lesson? Well, I guess it is the fine line
you must draw between the owners and the general manager.
We all won on that deal.

The rest of coaching? Much of it comes when I just tell the
story of the season.

Let's call it this.

The bounces.

And let's get into it with training camp, the merger, the

super bowl, the baby-sitters, the rich kids and the old man with the brain—Parilli. And the rest of them—the quarter-backs.

"Them."

8.

"Them"

DURING AL DAVIS' skyrocketing sixteen week tour as commissioner the developments moved as swiftly as a floating crap game. Davis was all ideas, moves, attacks, intrigues. One of his wildest—if not his brightest—was to capture the quarterbacks of the National Football League.

Any player in either league can play out an option, taking the automatic cut, playing the extra year and then joining a new team.

With the infighting going on, some of them were doing just that. It would be preposterous to assume that the players were sacrificing any money, because very obviously they would get their loss—and a little something extra—in next year's pay check from the franchise to which they were switching.

The Patriots didn't have any jumper. Nor did we solicit any, and therefore we weren't in on any of the intrigues. No club is going to tell anything they may be doing privately.

Davis, however, now began circulating the league with his plan. The war chest would be used to cripple the N.F.L. by buying up their key quarterbacks for 1967. There were definite impressions that Rudy Bukich of Chicago, Jim Ninowski of Cleveland, Washington's Sonny Jurgeson, Milt Plum from Detroit and Fran Tarkenton from Minnesota would be coming over.

Oakland had already signed Roman Gabriel from the Rams—you might know Davis would start the idea with his own team—and Don Klosterman, who was reviving the riddled Houston franchise, had allegedly presented a written offer of $750,000 over ten years to John Brodie of the San Francisco 49ers.

The deal didn't go through, of course. But Davis—and Lamar Hunt, the chief architect—were in there trying and you can't tell, it might have had some influence on the N.F.L. in helping the merger. Certainly, the N.F.L. quarterbacks weren't going to complain. It put them in a great bargaining position on their own team contract negotiations.

Frankly, the idea had both its merits and its drawbacks. There were weaknesses on some A.F.L. teams. On others, we had good quarterbacks who were fully capable. Davis' theory, however, was only to strip the N.F.L. of its key men, knowing full well that it takes years to train a good quarterback.

If we are to discuss football in depth, then, it becomes important to completely register the importance of the quarterback. And his development.

Come along then. Let's take a look at them.

"Them."

The quarterbacks. The different ones.

Count "them" off on your hands. The great ones. Graham. Waterfield. Unitas. Layne. Tarkenton. Ryan. Starr. Parilli. Namath. Kemp. Dawson.

That's ten.

Grow another hand. Count the ones who came along when football wasn't the child of television. Luckman. Christman. Eddie LeBaron. Frankie Albert. Baugh. Maybe a couple of others.

What does it take to be a professional football quarterback? I suppose, really, it could best be said as follows.

Give me a quarterback who:

1—Knows how to snatch victory from the jaws of defeat . . . all by himself, with his reputation on the line. And keeps his mouth shut if it doesn't work because someone forgot a block, or because some end counting next year's pay check tried just a little less than hard.

2—Knows how to keep trying while watching defeat snatched from the jaws of victory.

3—Believes so much in himself that no matter what happens he will hang around in this game, still trying to prove himself, until the time comes when he does.

4—Is tall and throws right-handed (you can't do without the latter). Albert was the only one who ever threw left-handed. LeBaron was the only small one that came along. A few get away with sidearm throws. But not many. The game has advanced to the point where you have to be fairly tall, a river boat gambler with the ability to take orders, a man without any fear, and a right-hander. You have to be right-handed and able to throw up and far because the ball spirals differently. Now, let some five foot eight southpaw come along and make me a liar. But it is a fact.

I'm lucky. At least I knew them all. From the moments in the huddles when they said the words, punched the quitters, cast the challenges, to the moments when they stood there all alone with a back foot planted and with about a thousandth of a second to hit the bull's-eye—without giving a thought to the fact that they were targets themselves.

It sound trite to say, but these are men who live like every game was their *High Noon*. A rare breed. Sometimes a breed of complete and utter depravity. This would be included in the chapter: "Quarterbacks I have known who wouldn't be allowed to take my dog out."

That chapter won't be written. They don't stay long.

This is just a book about average men, doing one thing better than anyone else. There is no glory in it. It is a business coupled with some innate desire that makes men want to live doing it—even when they know they may die.

If you were to equate the great quarterbacks with history, you might discover a sociological parallel. Perhaps, in another time, a quarterback would have been the flank commander in the charge of the Mongols, the laughing rogue with the earring who exec'd on the pirate ship Jean Lafitte, the lead scout on a Special Forces mission in Southeast Asia.

It takes something rare. Experience. Desire. Confidence. The absolute man.

For money, marbles, for practice—or even just for kicks—they'll try to beat you. The great ones. Then they'll do other things that are so childish that you can just sit back and laugh and cry at the same time in exasperation.

But that's what we make them. We demand the best. When they don't give it we throw them out. They live in a very lonely world where everyone waits for them to do magic. When they fail, everyone who reads a sports page or watches TV or buys a ticket knows it. When they succeed some coaches take credit, or the defense, or the offense. Only they and the coach will ever really know.

The quarterback in pro football is the ultimate in the star system.

In the United States we demand a tremendous amount from our stars. They are always on. They must always perform. But we never think about the time when they go offstage. They have the same worries everyone else has. Sometimes they explode.

One thing is certain. You can't make a team without a quarterback. And they don't grow on the branches of colleges. With very few exceptions they are men who have taken the hard knocks of life.

Johnny Unitas was getting three dollars per game (not six dollars as they say, just three dollars; the six dollars was for a championship) playing sandlot football after he blew his first shot in the N.F.L. Then Baltimore picked him up again and he became great. Snarling. Fierce. Put him in a football suit and he is a fantastic tiger. Put him off-field and he is quiet and calm and calls everyone but the water boy "sir."

Yet, as I write this, I know one thing Unitas must always live with. Going against Green Bay this year, in a game he never had a chance to win, trailing down the stretch and running out the string in the rain, Unitas fumbled the ball. He may know and they may know and I may know that he was never going to make it anyway. Someone missed a block. The ball was wet. The aging hands didn't close just right.

But this winter Unitas lives with the fact—he fumbled the ball. You can take all the other games and pour them into your grandmother's slipper. Because this will be the winter of the season he fumbled the ball.

It is the life of a quarterback.

A few stories. Because it is my game. This is how it was. The riverboat gamblers.

All sizes and shapes. There are the Cadillac quarterbacks. Like Sid Luckman. Somehow I always knew Sid would wind up in one. But he was a beautiful thing to watch in action. Sid would cut you up the middle and smile. He was completely and utterly merciless. That is what they pay off on. He had, like all good quarterbacks, the enormous ego of knowing that he could do it better than anyone else. For many years there was no one better.

Then there was Bobby Layne. Layne broke in as a rookie on the Bears when I was there and had no chance. Luckman. Johnny Lujack. And the kid with a Texas accent. Nothing. Layne was on his way home before he arrived.

Then it happened. Layne finally went to Detroit and found his level. The wild ones. Bobby ran them like Morgan the Pirate. Sometimes you would swear they were playing for gold doubloons instead of money.

Right down your throat, baby.

Ol' Bobby had plenty of experience as a loser. From the Bears he went to an ex-Boston franchise. Failing as the Yanks in Boston it moved to New York and became the Bulldogs. The only thing that was the same was the owner—Ted Collins, manager of Kate Smith. Collins tossed a couple of million down the drain of a dream called pro football. He was so unwelcome in New York that he once played a game with Pittsburgh before 221 people. Art Rooney owned Pittsburgh. Collins grabbed him in the stands and said, "Look, Art. You forget your share of the gate and let's throw the people out. We'll have them play a whole game just for you and me."

Brilliant. I love the taste of that. The line I love best,

though, was Layne's describing New York. "It was okay," he said. "The only trouble was, every time it was payday you were worried Kate Smith might have a sore throat."

Then came Detroit. The pieces went together. Championship. Did they buy just a nobody? No. They bought this one man. Standing in the huddle, two minutes to play, trailing by 3 points, 80 yards to go. "Gen'men," he said, "you block. He'll go right. I'll go left. He'll go down. I'll throw for a touchdown."

Championship.

The quarterback who was nearly crippled when Sam Huff smashed into him. He called the next play carefully, stepped back and threw right into Huff's kisser and knocked him out.

Great. Except the coach must have died a little because he wasted the down.

We place the pressure on the quarterbacks. There are those who will stand up at the Monday luncheons and mince their words and say sorrowfully, "We're terribly sorry to hear that their quarterback had a broken collarbone. We didn't mean to hurt him."

Baloney.

I can honestly say that I have never tried to hurt one since I became a coach. In the violence of the game as a player it was normal. The name of the game is hit the quarterback. As a coach I have to face one thing. Every defensive play fits into the piece of a puzzle which has one hole. Through that hole is supposed to go one huge man to hit that quarterback as hard as he can.

Not that we are heartless. There is a ground rule. If the quarterback breaks his arm pick him up gently. Then pat him on the rump to show sportsmanship, while sending him off towards the hospital.

For this is the violence game. Make no mistake about it. The only reason they have a penalty called "roughing the passer" is that good quarterbacks are too rare. And the only time we get mad at a penalty called "roughing the passer" is when a lineman wastes it.

We never set out to hurt anyone. But the quarterbacks are all alone out there and some of them have developed different methods of protecting themselves; of stopping massive men, of giving back as good as they get if it gets too rough and goes beyond the hard smashes which are their normal lot and extends to the vicious.

We put a lot of pressure on quarterbacks. We demand things of them. They talk about rookies becoming pro quarterbacks and stars. With the exception of Namath—name me one. The strong survive. They survive all the knocks and the hard times and this permeates way down deep in their bones and they get better. They survive. They know. Only then are they great. Passing scenes, little cameos to hold before the eyes. Here, then, blink, gone. A remembered scene in a living room on an afternoon. And gone. Four great years, five at the most. Forged amidst violence.

When the great one goes it is hard. The entire team must adjust. The coach may talk and praise and hope—and sometimes believe—but deep in his heart he knows it is over and this year's schedule is to teach the new one how to take the knocks so that he can go on next year to try to be one of the great ones.

What does it take? From the moment of the training camp it takes that one ingredient—the thing that makes a quarterback. I don't know what it is. But I know the scenes.

They come into camp the biggest moneymakers. The stars. They know that somewhere ahead of them is that one moment when they are going to stand looking for a downfield receiver with 1,200 pounds of brain concussion coming at them. They know, if they are good, that they will stand there and then throw it.

Touchdown.

Everyone else in the camp will know it too. The squad always has one third string quarterback in camp. A good one. Sometimes a great college star. The minute he sees the old pros he knows. They share the secret between them. The innate knowledge that in this trade you can only make it the hard way. People only see them standing among dirty uniforms all spick and span and clean on Sunday afternoons. They forget the years which brought them there.

Things like your quarterback coming back with two teeth missing. "What happened?"

He says, "That- ——you have playing right tackle only knows one block. It's called, 'Look out, Babe.' "

Rather than go tough against the other guy, the right tackle is alibiing out there. Yelling over his shoulder to cover, "Look out, Babe," and the quarterback is going down like a big lump of misused dirt, mashed from his blind side.

The quarterback isn't going to alibi. When he comes back to the sidelines he already is able to take care of himself. He knows. He looks at you and he says it—and only you and he will know it—*your* right tackle."

By the end of the season there is a new tackle. It is an unwritten agreement between coach and quarterback. There is the coach on the field. This is the quarterback. There is the coach on the sidelines. The man on the sidelines is powerless. He has planned. Only the coach on the field will execute.

Some come tough into training camps. Some don't. The latter leave.

Christman came to the Cards. I forget the quarterback's name.

Christman had been away to the wars for four years. The other had the job sewed up. He said, "What do you play, Christman?"

Christman said, "Poker, pinochle and pitch. What do you play?"

From that moment on, Christman had the job.

The Jets paid $400,000—give or take a Lincoln Continental—to Joe Namath. And $200,000 to John Huarte—give or take a Cadillac. Weeb Ewbank—and the team—heard one conversation. Huarte called Namath, "mister" when he met him. It was polite. But it was over. Namath had the job. Weeb later said he picked him at that moment.

The quarterback is paid for one reason—to lead. Regardless of the circumstances. He may come from another place. He may be a journeyman. He may have learned the trade in the far-out places. He may be playing the string out. Who knows what is in the deep recesses of his heart? The coach must hope—and hope he can touch it. And hope he will respond.

If he does, then for that three or four years he will come into your living room and stand there in the spanking white pants directing the violence game. Then he will be gone again. But you'll remember. Because you saw greatness.

Picking a quarterback is a match-up. There are times when he is going to be defiant. It is a declared truce, really. It is one man's mind against another's. The coach must prove he is right. The quarterback must go with him in the clutch. He will only go if he believes. And the coach can only go with him if he believes. A declared truce.

The quarterback drives ten men, anyone of whom on a given day could make him an old man with one punch. The quarterback is always driving his ten mules with the certain knowledge that there is someone younger—and potentially better—sitting on the bench with the headphones who might come in to replace him.

That I suppose is another unwritten rule of pro football . . . never give the job away. When I was a pro they could never get me out of there. Sick, hurt, a mound of jelly, I was going to play. Because I knew one thing—when I came out someone else went in. If he was good enough—even lucky enough—he got the job. I was out.

That is another basic rule of the professionals: only the strong survive. I guess it is why we have that emptiness of never making any real friends on the team. They can't be permitted. It is the one luxury our sport does not allow.

The quarterbacks know. They sometimes are out there with only the shattered ligaments of an arm. An arm which will pain them on a cold winter's night. The coach may never know. The quarterback will never tell. He keeps his hurts to himself.

They know, too—and the coach does as well—that they are out there to do it. They will be out there and they will give a great season on a Blue Cross elbow and a Blue Shield knee. Perhaps they will even make a champion. Perhaps the ligaments and the cartilage went in the seasons when the team was building a franchise or a championship.

The years came and they were successful. Now it is the last one. The quarterback is out there throwing. Doing the best he can. At one moment the coach suddenly knows and so does the quarterback. Between seasons he is gone. Traded. Perhaps retired. But gone. Maybe he tries to play the string out. Maybe he succeeds.

An old friend of mine, Tobin Rote, did. I don't think he will take this amiss if I say that in his last days with San Diego everyone knew he was looking for ways not to run with the ball. He was an old, old man. But he knew how to do it. He beat Boston for the championship—he beat me for the championship—by a score of 51-10. I could only stand there on the sidelines and think, "Well, at least I made it to the finals. Darn that Tobin. I gotta respect that————for what he did."

Rote retired the next year.

Poetic justice.

With half a break we could have busted his arm.

No one would have felt worse than me. Like this season. Coach of the Year. Everyone says I am the nice guy coach. Very nice. I appreciate it. But who is kidding who? I never sent anyone out to kill anyone. Or hurt anyone. But it lies there. I know any time I harness all the violent poundage. Whether I reckon with it or not. The fact of the matter is that it is there. It is part of the forty-man weapon at my command.

It could happen.

Quarterbacks.

They come and they go. The rejects who become great. The rejects who quit. The college hotshots who don't have it. The college wild ones who make it and stuff it down your throat. The pros. The retired ones. Sometimes they are the greatest hazard of them all. The old ones who always tell how they won every game. They didn't lose a thing. It was always the guy that dropped the pass, the runner who slid when he should have slanted, the coach who didn't understand. Yet I want to embrace them, too. Hug them. Say, "Sure, baby, that's how it was." Because they were all part of it. Wars are more important. But this, in our infinitesimal way—viewed by 50 million Americans every Sunday—is our war.

Oh, a coach can make mistakes about quarterbacks. Bad ones. Even Paul Brown did. He drafted a college quarterback to come in behind Otto Graham. Beautiful. The movies were great.

There was only one problem.

He stuttered.

"Th-th-th-irty-th-th-th-hree."

That's a delay of the game penalty right there.

No mention of quarterbacks would be proper without Otto Graham. There's an analogy here, as well. Graham came along in the old All America Conference. The N.F.L.— a poor relation of the current N.F.L.—looked down their noses at the Cleveland Browns. Nothing.

Otto and the Browns came over in that merger. Zip. Championship. Zap. Championship. No one scoffs anymore.

Look for the same thing with the N.F.L. and the A.F.L. They have only one thing on us—the Canton Bulldogs were their direct antecedents. We took a short cut.

Otto was superbly great. He could do it all. My quarterback, Babe Parilli, incidentally, played behind Otto with the Browns.

For Paul Brown. Parilli left early.

Ultimately, Graham himself quit when, as he said, "the tensions became too great."

Interesting analogy here. Both men were great quarterbacks. Brown was a great coach. But shouldn't a quarterback have the right to make some decisions on his own? Obviously, the lack of the right to make decisions—and the constant shuttling in and out of plays—had a strong effect on both Graham and Parilli.

Boston Record American—Sunday Advertiser

With Babe Parilli

    This is probably as good a time as any to put to rest the thought that professional coaches make all the decisions for their quarterbacks. This is simply not so. Perhaps Paul Brown gave us all a bad name. Sometimes you will see a man scuttling in with a play. More often than not he is just replacing a man who is winded. As you sit there thinking, "Here comes the play," it very often is only a case of giving someone a rest.

    We have what we call the game plan—something we will discuss later—and basically we go with that. I won't deny that from time to time the assistant coaches in the press box find something and call it down. But these circumstances are rare. The quarterback must be trusted. He must call the shots. If he becomes just a puppet on a string then it is just one more time like Paul Brown. Otto Graham summed it up best of all. "I used to try to change the play," he said once. "Then I just quit. It was easier the other way."

But that wasn't football. It was—what did Graham call it?—tensions.

Which brings us back to my quarterback, Babe Parilli, who darn near had fits the first year he played for me.

To go back to the beginning, Parilli is the perfect example of a quarterback who had to experience failure to achieve greatness. An old Pennsylvania boy (he was all scholastic at Rochester, right across the river from Joe Namath's Beaver Falls—two years after Joe Willie was born), Parilli had all the marks of a man who would become a legend.

Bear Bryant had him at Kentucky (it's amazing how these same names keep recurring, isn't it?) and they tabbed Parilli "the Sweet Kentucky Babe." He was twice an all American, led the team to the Orange, Sugar and Cotton Bowls. Green Bay picked him in 1952. Babe was the logical man to restore the franchise. He fell right on his face. Two years in the Army made him the forgotten man and Green Bay traded him to Cleveland to come in behind Graham. It was one of those trades that isn't a trade. If he didn't make it, then back to Green Bay.

Parilli didn't have a chance to make it. Paul Brown called the shots. The only things that happened to Parilli were a bad case of the hives and a series of sessions with a psychiatrist.

The Babe was nearly ruined. He returned to Green Bay in 1957—a season distinguished by one victory—and then Lombardi came along, looking for winners. He had Bart Starr and Parilli. Starr stayed. After 1958, Parilli wasn't even wanted on any other N.F.L. team and wandered north to play in Canada.

Typical of this tight little island called football—Starr himself was a kid who once put pictures of Parilli on his bureau. As a college freshman, he was sent to Bear Bryant's training camp at Kentucky to learn from the Babe and for three weeks the Babe taught him the finesse of being a quarterback. Now, years later, Starr was driving Parilli out of a job.

Parilli wound up at Oakland in the first year of the American Football League. In the off-season we traded for him and after the fifth game in 1961 I became head coach.

So what did Parilli walk into? A two-quarterback alternating system, just like Brown had. Butch Songin—who would have stayed and become great if he were only younger—was one quarterback and Babe was the other. There was one difference between my style of coaching and Brown's. I put in two quarterbacks because neither was completely sure enough of himself to make a series of continuing decisions.

Songin would call one play, while Parilli observed from the sidelines. Then Parilli would go in and call the play he had decided on while Songin was thinking. Then they'd switch again.

Sort of like a Scotch twosome in golf.

The funny thing was that it worked. We somehow made a connection and down the stretch were 7-1-1 and chased Houston right to the wire for the title. The only thing was that Lemm never lost a game, so we couldn't catch up. With three games to go, Songin was injured. Parilli had the job at last.

Neither one of them had ever complained to me personally about the system of coaching, but I could watch them both flinch sometimes. That's what they pay me to be a coach for. Let 'em flinch. Test them. Fire them. Put them on the line. See if they have it. Halfway through the season I knew one thing—Parilli was no failure. He had become a quarterback.

Next season he really was and for the first time received the recognition he deserved. He was all league quarterback and had the world on the end of a string—the string of the long bomb, the short hitch-pass, the cool, callous, nerveless direction of the professional. He drove that team and after nine games we were leading the division and headed for a title.

Then Houston broke his collarbone.

Deliberate?

No. Not to break his collarbone. But the name of the game is get the passer. They got him. It was over. The season ended with the Babe being dragged to the bench, looking up and saying very simply, "They broke it off, Mike."

That he came back is another story, which perhaps is best saved for the chapter entitled "The Bounces."

The Babe had become the ultimate quarterback, the prettiest thing in the world to watch in action. He would made mistakes. Sometimes they would be big ones. But he threw the mistakes over his shoulder carelessly and forgot about them and later on I'll tell you some stories about how a quarterback is supposed to handle his team in the heat of it all, how Parilli did it and, later, became M.V.P. of the 1967 All Star Game.

This is what we look for. This is what we pay them for. The wild ones. The ice-cold ones. They come to camp with different styles. One is called "Dandy" because, as he simply says, he is. Another comes back to the huddle snapping his fingers and humming a tune when things go well. Another runs his team like a warden and a fourth is so tough that if you argue he'll whack you in the mouth in the huddle and send you to the bench and right off the squad. Him or me. The other players will know that "me" the quarterback is going to stay.

They are rare ones. An old Boston College player, Ernie Stautner, summed it up when he was distributing violence for the Pittsburgh Steelers.

"I know those quarterbacks scare. I can see it in the corners of their eyes. And when I see it I want that quarterback to know that I am going for his face. I go out to let him know that I know he's scared."

If that happens, the quarterback is a walking dead man. Once the word gets out that they'll quit, that they're quitters, everyone in the world will go for the face.

Which is why I love this game. There's nothing as beautiful to see in action as a smaller quarterback, without any fear in the corner of his eyes, standing there watching the giants come after him and throwing the ball in the last split second for a touchdown.

Then, in falling, very carefully trying to keep a face mask out of his teeth.

Or, perhaps, just gently stepping on a hand.

9.
A Sound of Thundering Hooves

WHAT MAKES a team or a league? I can't really name it. It must be something instinctive among the participants. It is popular to compare professional football players to a herd of elephants charging with all the ferocity of a pack of lions and the acute knowledge of a bumblebee who only knows how to head in the direction of the honey.

Not so.

They fall somewhere in between.

I have to respect them. All of them. Some are just grown men with the pure souls of ten-year-old boys recently escaped from reform school. Others are men who would be brilliant in any field. To their credit, they chose football.

In between come those who are just passing through—big enough to do it, cowardly enough to fake it against smaller men or bigger, dumber men, willing to participate, but never daring to really take a chance. These are the half percenters. To the crowd in the stands they look like giants. To the team and to the coaches they are pygmies headed for the garbage can. A coach keeps his mouth shut about them. He sees them for what they are, uses them accordingly and then dumps them off on somebody else who needs a warm body to fill a big hole for a season or two. We never rap them because this

111

is pro football and some are only mercenaries. Some of us play it for sport. Some of us play for reasons of ego. Some of us play it because it is a way of life—these are the professionals. But always lurking in the background is the certain knowledge that you, the fan, pay a fiver or seven-fifty for a ticket—or buy a color TV and sit home—because you want to be entertained. The owners want you to be entertained and as long as we make you laugh, cry, sweat, angry, get excited, then we have a value.

When the intangible value passes, we are left with a ticket somewhere else: perhaps an understanding wife, maybe a crying kid or two who doesn't want to leave his friends in the third grade; an old supporter; a dog-eared scrapbook bulging with unfastened clippings you never quite got around to putting in place; two or three trophies; bad knees, bones that ache when the seasons change; the fear that you're getting too old—and it becomes a desperate fear—and another town, another apartment, another season.

Any wonder that the key to getting along in the pros is the simple code—never made a friend, never tip off a guy on the wrong moves, play it close and survive?

Yet, suddenly, you can take all of this and for one season, two—in some cases even three—you can weld it all together and made it a team. The team will be proud. The team will be valiant. The team will be exciting. Then it is gone and the coach must begin again.

A legend is a sometime thing. It is the Sunday morning sports page. Or Monday. The glimmer of one act on a shallow tube, one bit of violence or grace that comes into your home and is gone and the next day someone says, "Did you see that?" or years from now, if you are really lucky, someone digs it out of a corner and remembers and says, "I remember when you did so and so."

Which is much better than I can do. I guess it was Leahy who taught me. Last week's game, yesterday's game, last year's game. It is over and gone. In writing this book, I have had to search and search to try to remember even the big things. They just happened and then they were gone; because this is my trade. I work at it and if I am lucky each year I grow in it.

So this is the herd—the sound of the thundering hooves—and this is the story of one segment of them, a team called the Patriots.

Everyone else gets names like the Colts and the Giants and the Broncos and the Raiders and Packers. Well, when you come from Boston you have to count your blessings. They could have named us the Beans. As it turned out, Patriots suited us just fine, although we had hard times.

In the first place, we started like something out of a midsummer's nightmare suffered by a National Football League coach. You know how N.F.L. coaches are. They begin their season in July by driving to some exclusive boys' school in a Cadillac or a Lincoln. They greet their coaches like a corporate president. They have their trunks and their wardrobes. And a mystical aura which makes their pronouncements sound like something out of the handbook for greatness.

Now in the American Football League of this period (1960) we started out as best we could.

I put my one extra sports jacket in my tired B-4 bag. I checked my bankbook and found I had $9.11. My socks were best described as exhausted white and my rubber-soled shoes were more top and sides than bottom. The rubber was exhausted and the laces quit the second day.

Lou Saban was the coach. A good man. Joel Collier—right now on top of the heap—was one of the assistants. With glasses. A fate worse than death for a pro football coach. He didn't even have a record of playing as a pro. All he was can be simply put—a very nice, quiet, good, basically honorable gentleman of tremendous knowledge and no flair.

A man you would want for a friend. Anywhere except in pro football.

Billy Sullivan was the president of the Patriots. Which in those days was something like being squadron commander of a kamikaze flight. Joe Foss was the American Football League commissioner. Which was wonderful except when old Joe was gone hunting.

Sammy Baugh was coaching the New York Titans. Harry Wismer was the owner.

Al Davis was then at San Diego. A good guy not to play gin rummy with.

The remainder of the cast was, well, what shall I say? Would you believe—similar?

This was the wild time. McKeever—remember from the old college days—was back as general manager of the Patriots. We were opening up at Amherst on the grounds of the University of Massachusetts.

We opened with a bang. After all, it was the Fourth of July. After all, this was a league which would consider—and sometimes accept—players with names like "Cookie" Gilchrist and Joe Don Looney, of whom it can best be said that they were well named.

We were off and running. Mainly from the amount of talent we had. The idea was to keep moving and they wouldn't catch you. A football team? Listen. This was a football league that would make you consider suicide. If you could afford a hamburger you were afraid to go into the diner to get it for fear the cook would want to try out for the team. The bellhop put your one bag into the motel room (shared with two others) and you had better tip him good because the next time you saw him he might be your starting tackle.

Why kid ourselves? At that time—July 4, 1960—the American Football League was the dream of a band of desperate men who either had nowhere to go or were living on a hope. I believe the hope could best be described by the scene of shaving in the morning. The coaches would look in the mirror and would begin shaving. The first thought would be, "I hope I cut my throat."

We used to go to practice with the sincere thought, "No . . . no . . . I won't go through with it."

Patriots? The Minutemen were going to come back and start a brand new Revolution. Football? How can there be football when people come around with a set of sneakers and a rejection slip from the CANADIAN League? Not the pro league. We had guys come in with bad reputations from the Toronto Junior Canadian League. Two of them made the first squad.

Things were so bad that the coaching staff only knew one thing for sure. We would immediately be lynched after the people of Boston saw their first game. It would all be over that first night. The people would walk quietly down from the aisles with their ropes. They wouldn't even bother to hide their faces. They would just stalk down with their five dollar tickets sticking from their soft hats and we would stand there surrounded by bellboys and short-order cooks and Toronto Park League rejects, and without a word to anyone they would push the players aside and then they would hang us from the goal posts.

It was the same all around the country. Old pros who couldn't make it anymore were coming into camp and we were greeting them as though they were Red Grange. A quarterback connects on a 40-yard pass? Beautiful. This kid is a new Sid Luckman. (This kid couldn't be Sid Luckman if George Halas personally signed his birth certificate. Heck, this kid couldn't be Sid Luckman if Sid Luckman signed his birth certificate.)

Crazy. That first day we had something like 314 applicants. And we gave them all a look.

Then we looked at each other. So what is there to say? It's pro football, isn't it?

Pro football?

Are you kidding me, baby?

Gradually, the nightmare dwindled to only a bad dream. But there is no point in kidding ourselves. We were better than the pros were in the days of the Canton Bulldogs. There were times, though, when the Canton Bulldogs would have beaten us.

I point this out because there are many people who still sneer at the thought of the American Football League. In some circles it is the accepted thing to indicate that the American Football League is one step this side of a road show carnival which takes your money and runs. You throw the football through the hoop and the carney barker gives you a watch and then you find out the watch has everything but the mainspring.

Well, in a way they were right. In another they were wrong. We were a band of relatively desperate men. We knew baseball interest was ebbing.

We knew that the National Football League in the preceding six years had finally become big. And we knew the American Football League could be big. But we had to find the way to do it. Laugh now. We were lousy. But we had people who dreamed.

Example: Billy Sullivan, our president and the president of the American Football League. Billy had been big in the best days of college football. Billy had been big in the days of the Braves and the 1948 World Series team. Billy had taken his knocks and they were hard ones. But he knew at the start that if we could weather the first years we could make it.

I'll tell you about the opening years because I am not ashamed of them. They were hard, they were wild, they were so far out no one would believe all the stories. But they were based on a very real dream. I will also tell you right here and now and forevermore that the American Football League came of age. We can play and play well against anyone. The growth period was a lot shorter than it was for the National Football League.

The telling point, I sincerely believe, came when the N.F.L. finally decided to merge with the A.F.L. That tells the story. You don't merge with an opponent—business, sports, wars—unless you figure the caliber is equal.

Our caliber in 1960 was entirely unequal. Now it is different.

In these years—once we finally settled down and got the bellboys and the errant husbands and the short-order cooks out of the way—we were equal only to each other. As the years went on, our salaries went up. And our talent. Until now we are equal to any professional team.

I sincerely believe the Boston Patriots, for example, could have beaten Green Bay in this 1966 season. That, of course, is academic. But it is written before the Super Bowl Game. In fact this is all being written in the one week following our drive to the Jets game. We knew—and I still know—that we could beat Green Bay. Indeed, it might very well have been that they caught us looking towards Green Bay and not towards Namath. Or perhaps that is just a mental reservation that saves me from going completely mad.

Green Bay has a man that I have known well. We've been playing against each other for years. Back since I was a schoolboy. What is Green Bay? Just like the A.F.L. teams—a well-coached, disciplined team, with capable players at each position who do exactly as they are instructed. Gee, I had one play set up for Green Bay that would have fractured Vince.

Maybe next year.

That was our slogan in 1960. Next year. Oh, what a horrible year 1960 was. Poor Lou Saban had the courage of a man standing on the scaffold with the knowledge that if the trap didn't get him he would be electrocuted.

His instructions to his coaches were sound and good and were followed—pardon me, Lou, but it's true—with a sad smile which seemed to say, "And then, if this doesn't work, you cut my wrist and I'll cut yours."

Poor Lou wasn't even the first choice to coach. In point of truth, their first choice was Ben Schwartzwalder at Syracuse. Ben very wisely took a long look—maybe it was just a peek—at the American Football League and decided that he would remain at Syracuse. Otto Graham was next. He stayed at Coast Guard, but recommended an old Brown teammate. It was Lou Saban who put his neck on the line and came from Western Illinois. Bringing along a player, Larry Garron. Mark the name.

I liked Saban. He went to the executioner standing up. Then he went from being fired by the Pats to head coach at Buffalo and the American League championship. At the height of it all, he quit because he said he wanted to go back to the peace and quiet of college coaching at Maryland. In the last game of this book, Lou was coming back to Denver, which was trying to beat Buffalo. Denver beat me on a freak after firing Speedie because I beat him. Then split two with Buffalo, coached by Joe Collier, whom I beat twice. This was the same Joe Collier who was an assistant to Lou wearing glasses that first day in 1960 when the bellboys and the short-order cooks came after us at Amherst.

Confusing?

Not really. Just remember pro football is that way. Some of us survive. We are teammates in college or in the pros. Or we play for a man. Then we coach or play for. Then we play or coach against. Then we—well, you carry it out from there. I have my hands full trying to tell you what it was really like being in the world of football for twenty-five years.

Know one thing. For all of it, there is only one credo. Win. They don't pay off on losers and the rule is—never make so good a friend that you won't hand him his head if you have to.

Most coaches travel in teams. Both in college and in the pros. Hire a head coach and buy his personal team—his offensive line coach, his backfield coach, his defensive line coach.

As the years go on, some assistant coaches become good enough. They go to the coach and tell they have an offer and then they go on to become head coaches. There is one ground rule—never steal a coach for yourself who belongs to a coach who brought you along. Not because of secrets. Just because it somehow developed. Maybe it could be called an honest rule among men who inhabit a world of rogues.

Oddly, the world spins in different twists. You might be a head coach for a while and then find out you're not able to do it—or perhaps you just don't want to do it—and you revert to being an assistant. Quite often you go right back to the head coach and the team you once left. Is it regression? Returning to the womb? I don't know. But it happens. That's just the way this society has developed.

Observe, you'll see what I mean. But we also have another rule—never give the other guy even one percent of an even break. In the colleges you might let up on a coach if you have him beaten 48-7, and time is running out. In the pros the rule is to rack it up—always being careful, of course, to protect your stars for another day. The fans pay money to see the best and we must give it to them. You see, you can coach the team and all that, but you must protect your stars because sometimes in a game which is gone you might risk your key man and some 300-pounder with the emotion of the moment, or perhaps just a ten-year-old brain which registers only anger or joy, will twist his arm off or break his ankle. You can get mad as hell. But that doesn't bring the arm or the ankle back—and if it happens, then it is your fault, not that of the player, nor that of the opposing coach. Because you stuck your neck out. And they broke it off.

I point out all of this because there have been judgements, stories. I am sure you wonder. We have only these ground rules. For the rest you are on your own. To become a head coach in this business you have to recognize one thing—you were hired to be fired. Lose too much and they will fire you. Get fired and you will go home to the family and check the bankbook and be on the street looking for a job without too much money.

How's this for a job application—would you like to hire a forty-five-year-old ex-all American, who earns $50,000 a year and doesn't have a dime, but is very experienced in handling 280-pound wild men? This will get you a job in only two places—a zoo or on a hotel staff which needs a bell captain to handle 280-pound bellboys. I don't know many hotels that have bellboys that size.

Anyway, Saban had one tough thing to handle. He hired the staff. Except his personnel scout-backfield coach type, who was hired directly by Billy Sullivan behind the fence at Holy Cross.

This did not entitle him to love me. To Lou's everlasting credit, there was never a sign that he felt any differently about me than he did about all the rest of them. We were all in it together.

Nor was there any sign from Sullivan or McKeever that I rated any differently.

We all just put our heads together and shuddered and went to work.

Here they came—the thundering herd. And some old friends, too. Ralph Dello Russo, equipment manager with B.C. in my playing days, joined us. One of our most valuable possessions. Equipment managers can cause a team a lot of trouble. Quite often they'll be clubhouse lawyers—or else they'll deal in the sports black market, selling equipment to fans who specialize in adoring by buying a stray helmet or jacket.

Dello Russo was perfect. We owe him a vote of thanks for it.

Then there was John Fitzgerald, our business manager and our first season ticket customer, John Birch, who became a sales promotion man. That led to a crack which could sum up the Patriots in that first year. Someone—I think it was Milt Gross, a qualified commentator—wrote, "The only famous name the Patriots have is John Birch."

But we had some beauties, if not some names. The gypsies. The wrestlers. The wrestlers came from out of the woodwork. Every 250-pounder figured he had found a home. Gino Cappelletti was a football failure. A complete reject. But he didn't have anything else to do and he came along for the ride with a kid we drafted. The kid is gone. Gino is still the M.V.P.

Our big stars were to be Syracuse's Gerhard Schwedes and Ron Burton. Schwedes tried, but he was an all-round player and we needed specialists. Burton would have been one of the all-time greats, but he was unlucky physically. Everything happened to him.

We had a fullback named Wray Carlton. In the very first exhibition Carlton let up on a couple of line bucks. Saban didn't dig that. He traded Carlton to Buffalo for someone named Al Crow. Crow lasted one week and was cut. Saban— after he left Boston—went to Buffalo and won three championships using a fullback named Wray Carlton. And you think luck isn't part of this game of coaching?

Good kids. And beauties. Everyone was a stranger. There was no hazing. But there were gags. Jack Davis was a sometime wrestler. Another player was also a wrestler. Davis, who played several years, set it up one night. The two would do the act, in the dormitory TV room. There were thirty men sitting around, all complete strangers. All quietly watching TV.

The other wrestler got up and without asking flicked the dial. None of the twenty-nine made a move. All strangers. Then Davis got up, walked over and flicked the dial back. The wrestler got up and turned the dial again and all of a sudden it was *High Noon* and twenty-eight strangers were clearing out of the way of the showdown. For five full minutes they did the whole fight scene, broken furniture and all, and no one even tried to break it up.

Which shows you what kind of camaraderie we had that first year. Real team spirit. Huh. Yet later they took a gun from a man.

We staggered through it. And wound up in the bottom of the league.

Mostly with gags. Abe Cohen was a good devoted kid. In the exhibition season the players are paid off in cash in an envelope after every game. Their salary doesn't start until the season. In those days, it was fifty dollars a game. Abe was so anxious he told Ed McKeever he would play the game for green stamps.

After the next game Abe came out of the shower and stood in line to get his envelope. Green stamps. McKeever said, "Well, I just took you at your word, Abe."

The Green Stamps league.

Forgive me, Father Halas.

In 1961 we had better luck. Parilli came to us from Oakland. The Moon Man arrived. The Cowboy came. The team busted up a hotel in Denver and the cops arrived. San Diego's Keith Lincoln stole Gino Cappelletti's best shoes. All of a sudden it was a league and a team.

Parilli was our target all through that long summer. We had the tip on Babe in our first year exhibition game with Oakland. He was brilliant. Really great. But on the way out of camp, George Sullivan asked Eddie Erdelatz about him. "I've got better," Erdelatz said. If he did, his name was

Unitas. We knew then that there was trouble between them and set it up through a long series of phone calls. The trap was sprung. It was a major trade involving other players as well, but we had Parilli.

And the Moon Man. Awfully nice fellow. Except when the moon was full. He made no trouble. He just walked down to what Boston calls "the Combat Zone," and spent every dime he had in his pockets. Got in a fight . . . came home. In the full of the moon. We finally solved his problem by limiting him to $300. It saved wear and tear on a lot of heads.

The Cowboy was along the same lines. Quiet. Respectable. Very calm. Except Monday nights. Then he liked to race motorcycle cops. They couldn't get mad. After all, he was a cowboy wearing a white hat. We had to let him go finally because the interest on the bail bonds was more than the team treasury could afford. We lost around $600,000 the first year of operation. This second year didn't look like it was going to be much better and I got a tremendous boot out of it when the Giants' Jim Lee Howell called the A.F.L. "just a spoiled bunch of rich kids." Jimmy, are you kidding me? Were you putting me on? Perhaps I shouldn't laugh. I was offered a job with the Giants in 1960, but stuck it out.

We also picked up a trainer, Bill Bates. Our resident psychiatrist, and valued associate, of whom more later.

On Monday, October 10, the phone rang.

We were 2-3. Lou Saban and the rest of the assistants were going over game films for the Houston game coming up. The Patriots' lawyer—Bill Finucane—was on the phone. He asked me to come down to the office after practice. I asked permission from Lou, who said, "Sure."

It was four o'clock and Sullivan said, "Mike, I'm going to make a change this afternoon. Do you want the job?"

I said, "No. I don't want to steal a man's job."

Sullivan put it simply and to the point. "Mike, Saban is through. If you want the job take it because it doesn't make any difference at all. He's through anyway."

I guess this is where the years of experience come in. It is the cold hard fact of football. You are hired to be fired, to sit there and wait for the door to open and the man to come in. I had given Saban good service. Been loyal. I knew he wasn't getting along with McKeever, but I stayed out of it.

"Okay, Billy. If Lou is definitely through." Funny, a coach will never use the word "fired."

I went back up to the practice field. Saban was gone. In my absence he had been called downtown too. The door had swung open. The phone had rung.

My first job was to get ready for Houston. My first phone call was to Wally Lemm. I offered him the job as my assistant. "I can't, Mike," he said. "There's an announcement coming out tomorrow. I'm going to become head coach at Houston, either this game or next."

I got ready to beat Houston and Lemm. All our lives we dreamed of being head coaches in the pros. In our first game, we would be going at each other's throats.

The team accepted it well. Saban had lots of class. We shook hands and he left, later to take his staff to Buffalo, where he was to haunt me for years.

I called the team together and reached way back into my mind and tried to think of all the things Leahy would say, or Halas, or Walsh, or Myers. Something inspiring. All that came out was, "Okay, fellas. You're professionals. Stop horsing around. You can be a good team. Much better than the standings. Let's all work together."

Houston was 1-3 coming into town. We were 1-3-1. Friday night we played to a wild 31-31 tie and the race was on. For the rest of 1961 we chased Lemm. Parilli and Songin alternated at quarterback. Neither one liked the system, but I think it worked. I gave them very little advice. It wasn't the Paul Brown style. It was just to let them call a play and then think for one play. It must have worked somehow. We were suddenly a team. A team. Not just a bunch of strangers derided and booed by our own fans—a team.

The plane was pitching and yawing coming back from somewhere. A guy was joking on the intercom. "Okay, everyone out to the starboard wing for agility drill."

Parilli was going back for a pass against San Diego. A block was missed and Ernie Ladd was coming at him. Parilli couldn't get the ball away. Couldn't move. Parilli looked the six foot ten Ladd right in his wild eyes and yelled, "No, Ernie. No. No." It slowed him up just long enough for the Babe to bounce down more gently. Ladd went off shaking his head in shock. We had a slogan: "No, Ernie, no."

Cappelletti was on his way to his first scoring title with 147 points. He had a new name. "The Duke." The most beautiful wardrobe in sports. He threw a party at his apartment after a game one night and somehow San Diego's Keith Lincoln made off with the best of his twenty pairs of shoes.

The entire league waited to see what would happen. Meanwhile we bounced from town to town and from win to win. And Lemm kept going with Houston. Finally it was the last day and we were playing at San Diego. We flew into town underdogs. Gino didn't waste a minute. He went to the phone booth and dialed a number.

"You dirty————. Where are my shoes?"

Lincoln didn't even ask who it was. "I'll buy you a new pair, Duke. I've worn these out," he said.

Another funny story. An episode. But we were a team. We were supposed to lose to San Diego. We racked them, 41-zip. But, up in Oakland, Houston was also winning. The year was over. Lemm was the champion. At least we went home with our heads up. What made it a team? What makes a franchise? I don't know. A story. A funny scene. A catch phrase. Perhaps the two back-to-back games with Dallas. Cappelletti kicked a field goal with time completely gone and we won, 18-17 at Dallas. We went right back to Boston and beat them again, 28-21.

There it was. The Patriots weren't a joke anymore. Something touched them—and I know it wasn't me. It was themselves. They were proud. The thundering hooves weren't just a bunch of uncoordinated gypsies galloping by. They were in harness.

In 1962 we were going to win it all. We had placed a lot of all stars the year before, including Larry Garron. Not too much can be said for this very quiet, very charming man, who probably has more courage than anyone I will ever know.

In those three years—1961-62-63—he literally carried us right on his very small back.

Garron came to the Patriots at the very beginning. He had played for Saban at Western Illinois. Saban never forgot the way Garron played with broken ribs to win a game for him. In the highly competitive world of our first camp, Garron was on the spot. He was Lou's boy. The players hung a name on him, "Boardhands." They pressed him, made him drop passes and exploited the fact that he was a thin 165 pounds. In our fourth game, he played with a fever and looked horrible. After four plays, Saban put him on the bench, then called him later that night and told him he was cut.

Garron flew home to Boston and completely disappeared. He moved his wife and son into a cold water flat. The neighborhood was so bad that a man was killed on his doorstep. It broke his back, but not his heart. Saban sent out a telegram for him to join the team in pre-season camp in 1961. He came to stay, now weighing 195 pounds. He had some glorious moments. But the sight I remember best is Larry Garron trying to learn the one thing he lacked, the knowledge of how to block. He wasn't "Boardhands" any more. He was a member of the team. But to block he had to go against my man-eaters—Addison, Dee and Eisenhauer. The only way to learn how to block is against the muscle. They wanted to teach him. Standing there or charging and letting a 200-pounder block you is not always the most gentle gesture of friendship. Garron would slam into them and fall down. He'd be up and slam again and they'd give an inch. Gradually, he learned. I'll never forget the sight of him, with his nose all bloody and his hand scraped, running a one-on-one against Addison and knocking him down. Addison picked him up and said, "Atta boy, Lar. You're going great. You're learning."

Garron wiped the blood away and smiled. It was 1961 and he was a Patriot. Addison is a Southerner. Garron is a Negro.

Yeah, in 1962 we were a team and we were going to win it

all. They couldn't laugh at us anymore. Atlanta, New Orleans and Kansas City all wanted franchises. Sullivan put over a TV deal. We weren't solvent. But no one was going to chase us away. We played the first nationally televised A.F.L. game against Houston. Appropriately, it was the first pro game ever at Harvard Stadium. And the last. Tax problem. We were still looking for a good field. Meanwhile, we had to run the gauntlet at old Braves Field. From the locker room to the field. Right through the fans. Intoxicating. I don't mean that as a knock. They meant well. But these were all night games and it was cold and a little something on the hip didn't hurt. If we were winning it wasn't bad. But if we were losing at half time and came down the ramp they would give us the old bum-bum-bum and the breath. By the time we got to the bench we felt like we were half in the bag.

We didn't lose many at the start. By mid-season we had turned away 10,000 for a game with Dallas and we were leading the league by half a game.

We went to Houston (Lemm was gone then, moving to the N.F.L. and the St. Louis Cardinals). We were breezing and then Parilli fell back into the pocket and a block was missed and he was hit from his blind side.

My stomach turned when I heard the cr-r-unch. I knew he was hurt before I went out there. Huddle. Bates, the doctor, Holovak, the players, white-faced Parilli. "It's broken, Mike."

So was the season. My only other quarterback was Tommy Yewcic, who in all his career had only thrown eight passes. Gee, did he try. We lost, 21-17, and that only brought us to 1963. You don't win without an experienced quarterback. No championship.

In 1963 I learned several lessons. I had a player come to me for an advance. I gave him $3,000 during the off-season. Then, by chance, a good trade popped up. I traded him and when I asked for the three grand, he drew himself up and said, "Look. I don't have to give it back. You traded me. That cancels any deal I have with you."

Coaching lesson—never advance money to a six foot three giant with a ten-year-old brain.

I liked that man, though. He had an argument with another player once. The players had a party for their wives. This other fellow brought the best looking blonde shady lady you ever saw in your life. Now these giants may sometimes be fierce, but like all men who live in a world of violence they have a feeling for women. They took offense and the next day my traded player—let's call him Smith—turned to the escort of the lady of the evening—let's call him Jones—and said, "Jones, you gotta nerve bringing a woman like that to a wives' party." Jones took offense at this and they nearly went at it, but the whistle blew for practice and they trooped out. Jones wasn't at the practice. He had suddenly disappeared. He showed up back in the locker room.

With a great big gun. He pointed it in Smith's face and said very calmly, "Now, you ———. What were you saying to me?"

Dead silence. Sweat on the forelip. Then they all jumped Jones and grabbed the gun. I think if an official saw it he might have called a few personal fouls.

Jones was dumped right after that. Smith went off with my $3,000 advance. The gun is long since gone, too. I think Al Davis of Oakland, collector of Americana, still has it.

Anyway, it goes to show you what makes up a team. They must have had some cohesive feeling to go after Smitty with a gun. Or maybe he brought their date to the wives' party.

But 1963 was a vintage year. Parilli was better than ever. So was the team. We won the Eastern championship standing on our hands and went for the championship against San Diego. Did you ever have a bad day? Yeah. I know the feeling. San Diego beat us 51-10. I didn't even feel bad after the first 50 points. We were all fouled up. But at least we were in the championship.

The only thing we got out of that trip was laughs. We stayed in a beautiful hotel with a sunken bar behind which was a sunken swimming pool. On the street level, you were really on the second floor. One player brought his dad along. His father asked, "Where's the pool?"

"Right here, Dad," the player said, and threw him two stories down into it. Old Dad, poor Dad, came floating in front of those sitting there having a cool one. Since he weighed about 275 himself you have to admit it was a helluva throw.

The trouble with being around football players is that when they want to vent their enthusiasm on a nice sunny day they sometimes do strange things.

This same player was not a man to play favorites. Later he was sitting on a veranda. Someone pointed out a movie star to him. He walked over and said, "Gee, are you———?"

Satisfied with the answer, he smiled, picked up the star and threw him in the pool too. Sounds like something out of a Bobby Kennedy party at Hickory Hill.

Football players. They'll be the death of me.

In this game the beauties come with hairy legs instead of beards. But we'll probably someday have one expressionist like that, too. They are the last of the free souls, some of them.

They present a coach with some trying moments. How do you handle it? Laugh? Fine him? Trade him?

The Cowboy wore high heeled boots, no tie. The rule says that on the road, in hotels, the players must have a jacket, shirt and tie. "C'mon, Cowboy. Let's not get a nut name. This is a new league. Get rid of those boots and put on a tie."

The Cowboy took it well.

I met him in the lobby later. He was wearing the craziest rainbow necktie I've ever seen. And red painted toenails.

He pointed at the toes. "Patriots' red," he said.

An individual. I had forgotten to tell him to put on shoes.

Coaching lesson—laugh. Then step on his toes.

A trainer is an important part of a team. Part psychiatrist, part doctor, part housewife. He becomes as much one of them as any tackle or guard or quarterback. The only thing running against him is his size. He must give away weight in the horse play.

In San Diego—it must be something about the weather

there—the full moon was running some of their brains again. Gino Cappelletti was the ringleader. They pounced on poor Bill Bates and wrapped him in his sheet and spread and then taped him like a mummy and put him out in the hall. Bates bounced from wall to wall, seeking help. He found, finally, only a frightened manager, who untaped him. Bates professed his deepest thanks. The manager was gracious—he handed him a bill for sixteen dollars for a new spread.

We had a new member of our cast of characters—the Mummy.

Okay. 1964. I was made general manager. Someone said I was getting more money than any coach in the history of the league. Maybe. I was so busy I never did get around to signing a contract. Off and running again.

Fred Bruney, one of my coaches, had a chance to join the Eagles and I shook his hand warmly. He was a fine man. I signed Chuck Weber to coach with Art Spinney and Jesse Richardson. I've never been sorry. A good team, added to by Rommie Loudd.

Bruney had just finished building a house. Parilli bought it. Perhaps this will tell you a little something about the problems of a pro quarterback. The Babe married a girl from Green Bay, a former Miss Wisconsin. They had a nice little son. For seven years they had never felt secure enough to own a house. Each year they moved from apartment to apartment. Now the Babe was finally getting to feel secure. He bought a home and he was a beautiful thing to watch in action.

We went right down to the wire, our record 10-2-1, and be darned if we weren't tied for the championship with Lou Saban and Buffalo. We had to play them in a roaring blizzard at Fenway Park. Buffalo won 24-14 and went on to win the league title. Parilli was picked all League quarterback. Cappelletti was the M.V.P.

Holovak, in my book, was a horse's neck. You don't pay off on losers. I let them down somewhere. I started off scouting, started off on the long trips looking for some prospects. I needed a fullback. I needed a bodyguard, too, since this was the time to go into the bidding against the National Football League. Unfortunately, I couldn't afford a bodyguard. The price was too high.

As were all prices in those days while franchises bid themselves into bankruptcy trying to keep kids from the other league.

I knew what we needed. A fullback. I lucked out. I found Jim Nance. Old "Papa Bear" Halas and the N.F.L. were left moaning about this one—one of the few that got away.

That's the subject of another chapter. Turn now to a story of pure sportsmanship between leagues.

10.

The Bandit Kings

ROMMIE LOUDD calls football "the American Ballet." It is a pretty and true expression. No one yet has come up with a phrase which would express the fight between the American Football League and the National Football League.

Maybe it should be described as "the Rich Kids." Or, better still, "the Bandit Kings."

Everything conceivable happened. Here came all that huge beef out of college. Red shirts. Seniors. Hulking and strong. Here came the lawyers and the accountants in their pinstripe suits, carrying their twelve-page no-cut contracts.

Now what chance does a football coach or a general manager have in a deal like that? The smartest thing that either league ever did was to merge. Otherwise, we would have all gone into the barrel. You can't make a profit when you're buying half a million dollars worth of talent every year in bonuses. The contracts had to be no-cut, which meant that we could very often be stuck with a big man on campus who had absolutely no desire to risk his very wealthy neck trying to put a block or a tackle on some penurious peasant.

Everyone was in on the deal. The National Football League set out to impede the American Football League. There was talk—and I think it was with foundation—that C.B.S. was also throwing in some money for the war chest to secure the best entertainment for their channels.

Then, the A.F.L. pulled the rug out from under them in that long, secret meeting—no one will ever know what really went on—which resulted in the N.B.C. television deal.

Suddenly, it was even up. The N.F.L. could still try, but they couldn't push us over. We had danced and pirouetted along the precipice of oblivion, but we were back in action.

The wild time was beginning. Sickening. A kid wasn't a football player anymore. He was 250 to 275 pounds of all American buildup who was going to exact his own pound of flesh for signing. We could blame them? We signed with the N.F.L. for $500 and a train ticket in 1946. Now players wouldn't even travel to the team. You went to them—hat in hand.

It was—very naturally—vicious. So is a Presidential election. I'm not going to fault anyone for it. Everyone had reasons. Depending on the various franchises, the teams went to different lengths to get their men.

One move was to put college coaches on payrolls as area scouts. Don't misunderstand. I am not saying all college coaches were on payrolls. I am saying that some—using their own mature judgment, right or wrong—did accept such positions. Some teams had as many as forty-two. In both leagues. This can really help, especially if you are going after the coach's best player. You'll find opportunists anywhere.

Most teams used bird dogs and some refined it down to using private detectives.

I am sure that the reader is not so naïve as to assume that a huge twenty-two-year-old boy would not greatly enjoy lavish attention, private planes, pretty girls in mink coats, and at the end of the rainbow of this very real dream, a check for anywhere from $35,000 to $400,000.

The leagues worked in two fashions. One was the individual routine of the clubs; the other was the joint collusion of all teams under the direction of league headquarters. The idea was to keep the talent away from the A.F.L.

We worked just as hard. I am proud to say—and I really mean this, really proud—that the Patriots did not resort to the lengths used by others.

We tried to play it straight. We lost some. Not as many as you might think. But some that hurt. Some that were already signed before they were even draft eligible. The method was very simple. Put a binder up with a kid by the excellent expediency of giving his father a new house, a new job, a gift in cash. They had him locked in and, when he was publicly eligible, he might listen, but he was already gone.

It happened to us. I talked with a kid for a long time. I offered more than the best that the National Football League team gave him. He assured me he wasn't signed. He went downstairs for breakfast, was hoisted right out of the hotel and announced his signing to an N.F.L. team at another hotel.

It happens.

You just smile and shrug. The funniest thing was that most of those kids didn't make good anyway. They had two year no-cut contracts and that was it. After two years they were gone. They didn't play enough to earn it; they didn't have the drive; they fell out of shape, lost their confidence and were gone. Just another fooolish bonus boy. A joke. The tough veterans had a way of taking care of their own.

Some stayed. Some were so tough that they were a cinch to make it anyway. Joe Namath. Make no mistake. Joe Willie received his $400,000. Perhaps not all in one year—which would have been foolish, anyway, because of taxes—but in various incentive stages. It was worth it to Werblin. It was a darned smart move.

McKeever was our director of player personnel and as coach-general manager I followed the circuit. All winter, all, spring, traveling from town to town looking at films in various colleges; talking to coaches, to players; checking lists; going to games on Saturdays during the regular season. Trying to pick.

Both leagues held secret drafts. The public draft is held in November or December. In 1964 and 1965 the American Football League held a telephone draft much earlier. Everyone picked the players they thought they could get, both the seniors and the red shirts. (As a brief explanation, a red shirt is a player with an extra year of eligibility who would ordinarily be a senior. His red shirt comes from one season on which he is not a varsity member—hence, he wears a red shirt to identify him as a non-varsity participant and may do everything but play in the game. Thus, he may miss one season and be a five year student. However, by the rules of professional football the red shirt must be drafted in the year in which he would normally graduate. Red shirts are picked on a separate list and are more of a gamble since the player may be injured, or fail the pressure test of his senior football year.)

I am sure that the N.F.L. did the same. There were more bird dogs around bumping into each other than there were players.

The telephone draft worked to a degree. It also backfired. A case in point—oh, what a beautiful case—is this year's American Football League Most Valuable Player, James "Bo" Nance.

In mid-season, 1964, we held a secret telephone draft and New York picked Nance. Syracuse was coming down to New York to play Army at Yankee Stadium and after the game, Weeb Ewbank entered the locker room to say "Hello." Nance turned all future negotiations over to his attorney, a very fine—and I must emphasize this—a very fine attorney.

His name is Alan Brickman and Weeb, as I understand it, dealt basically through Mr. Brickman. There was a very strong rumor that the Chicago Bears had Nance sewed up, that Halas had locked him in a long time ago. New York didn't let up. It is just possible that they pressed too hard. Matt Snell was on his way to Rookie of the Year as a fullback. Whoever represented the Jets implied to Nance that they would be making a halfback out of Snell and moving Nance to fullback.

With a proud athlete, this is exactly the wrong thing to do. Never treat him as if he is stupid. Later, Nance said, "I didn't mind the competition of fighting Snell for the job. But thinking I was stupid and telling me Snell was going to be moved? Well, anyway, I didn't like that routine."

New York finally gave up and decided not to waste the pick in the regular public draft of late November. They threw Nance back into the pool and wrote him off as going to the Bears, or at least to the National Football League in pursuit of Jim Brown's record.

Dissolve now to my hotel room in Houston—the one time that town was lucky for me. We were telephoning our picks to the draft center in New York the night before the last game with the Oilers.

On the nineteenth pick, Billy Sullivan and I were leafing through my remaining index cards. Jim Nance, Syracuse.

Sullivan said, "Look, I know the stories about the Bears having him signed up. The Jets must know something. But what the heck, this is number nineteen. We aren't going to get much anyway. Let's take a chance. Time is running out. Take a chance."

I mumbled for a second. Then I said into the phone, "Jim Nance, Syracuse."

And we stole him.

The Bears picked both Gayle Sayers and Nance—and you can imagine how the "Papa Bear" would have done with that combination. Since this was still the days of the big raids, it was a matter of interest to see what would happen.

Unbeknown to us, Tom Stephens of the Patriots, a Syracuse graduate, had returned to the school every year for the alumni game and had talked up the A.F.L. and the Patriots. We didn't know it, but this was a big edge—even bigger than the lure of Brown's N.F.L. rushing records.

Finally, I called him and he said he thought he would sign. Just like that. Next Mr. Brickman called me and said Jim was going to wrestle (he was a collegiate wrestling champion) and I said, "Well, Mr. Brickman, if there's no rush, I'll be up in the spring."

I always make the spring training circuit through key colleges and one of my last stops is always Syracuse and Ben Schwartzwalder. I was determined about one thing—and this doesn't make me a Boy Scout—but I was not under any circumstances going to sign an early contract and put it in the drawer and let Nance wrestle when he was already signed. Nance and Mr. Brickman felt exactly the same way.

At the coaches' convention in Chicago, I ran into George Allen of the Bears. George said, "Mike, when are you going to talk to Nance? You ought to make your pitch."

Finally in late January I went up and we had a long talk. Later we talked on the phone and Nance said very honestly that he was going to visit Chicago. It went that way for a while and then we talked again—by this time it was "Bo" and "Mike"—and we discussed specifics.

Still no signing. In late March Nance won the wrestling title. His season was over. I scooted up to Syracuse early and we signed a deal.

Schwartzwalder told me, "He has a tendency to put on weight. But you keep him down under 230 and you'll have a great football player."

Old Ben was right.

The best thing, though, was that there wasn't any subterfuge in this deal. It was clean and neat and aboveboard. It stands both the player and the coach in good stead as the pro years go on. When you don't intrigue over money you have a better relationship.

At that, it required a full season and a little of the "psych" to make Nance a fullback. All the potential was there. He had a no-cut contract, I'll admit that. But he also had the desire.

There were, of course, others who received no-cut contracts. One was guard Dick Arrington from Notre Dame, whom we red-shirted in 1964, and another was Jim Boudreaux, a tackle from Louisiana Tech, who was our second choice in 1965. Both showed up for training in July, 1966, and before the first game in September I cut them from the squad. They still drew their money and were on the so-called taxi squad, but they were not on the team. They just weren't ready. Maybe next year.

I hope so.

It was a difficult decision. We needed linemen badly.

There was also the consideration that in the battle for beef we had gone to extraordinary lengths, making all kinds of press announcements about how great these draft choices were.

Any general manager who no-cut contracts a guy, lays out a lot of money—and I mean really serious money—and then cuts the rookie can have his head handed to him by the fans and the press. Who can blame them? I'm lucky my head wasn't handed to me by the owners.

But I have to face the men who make up my squad. I knew it wouldn't really be fair to force them to play with a man who wasn't well enough prepared or eager enough to play pro football.

I cut Arrington and Boudreaux.

Wow! You'd think I had stabbed Mother. I'd do the very same thing again. Arrington and Boudreaux still are contracted and they'll be back again next year. If they don't have any greater desire then I'll cut them again. That is the way it has to be.

This is one of the lurking dangers of a no-cut contract—the same old "psych" danger I faced when I loafed with Los Angeles in 1946—and it was one of the things that might have ruined both leagues.

The merger saved both of us.

Joe Foss had been our commissioner in the formative days, and a man with his war record and reputation was perfect for the job. Now it was time to fight for our lives and the owners picked a new commissioner—Al Davis, the old Oakland Raider coach and general manager.

Al has his moments. Yet for this time he was the perfect choice.

I've always thought that if you were involved in a war, then Al Davis would be the perfect choice for guerrilla chief. He harried the N.F.L. for sixteen hectic weeks.

At the blowoff, Davis didn't want to quit. He was certain he could make a better deal; he was certain we had the other league running scared, at last. Davis was ready to keep the pressure on. He opened his own special department and portioned out one paid professional bird dog to each team. They were to operate just like the N.F.L. did.

The rug was pulled out from under him. The leagues merged. Davis went home to Oakland crying "foul."

I was crying a little, too. In the sixteen weeks that Al was there he gave us a lot of fun, a lot of bills; and I was stuck with the bird dog. I didn't need him now that peace had arrived.

But Al always took the long range view. And you know, I've never yet even seen the bird dog?

Still, who knows? It might have been a good idea at that.

Anyway, look on the bright side. We merged and we solved the civil war and we got these nice healthy athletes out of the roadhouses and out of those Cadillacs and back into the nice fresh air of the playing field.

Well, you know what they say about pro football. That's the way the bonus bounces.

11.

The Bounces

YOU WILL notice now, on occasion, the use of italics and will sense from time to time a change in tense.

Because this is one season, one quick six months which are the breath and the lifeblood and the pulse and the wild raging storms and the laughter and the lingering sad minutes which make up all our lives.

In the other pages there were stories and there was a history of the twenty-five years I have known in pressure football.

This is the big season.

This one.

This is the way it went. For one person. Me. Mike Holovak. I cannot speak for the others, nor would I wish to.

I'm still trying to think of a title for this book. When we started it was supposed to be *Pro.* Then we thought about *In Hot Blood.* Halfway through the year it became *To Die by Inches.*

Maybe we just should have settled on *Untitled; Clinical Wavelengths from the Brain of a Football Coach.*

Some linemen would change that to read: *My Head Hurts from the Bounces.*

And this is the story of my bounces.

My team.

My friends, my associates, my enemies, the tigers of the jungle which we have chosen.

A jungle entered through the medium of a small square screen and people who watch it calmly, emotionally, regularly on Sunday afternoons in their living rooms.

A jungle entered through a turnstile with a ticket and a blanket and maybe something warm in a container.

A jungle entered through the screams of those who seek to be the biggest tigers. Their screams really aren't too different from the cries of the birds in the green decay I left behind in New Guinea so long ago. Or the silent screams perhaps of a man or a woman who watches it, venting an emotion to cleanse another, deeper emotion.

But to enter our world, you must come in with our screams, our talk, because this is the vast backdrop to our work.

It is a world of these sounds, this kaleidoscope of crushing bodies and crying voices:

"Ball . . . ball . . . ball. . . .

"Get set, defense. . . .

"Ready field goal team. . . .

"Hit him . . . hit him . . . hit. . . .

"Draw . . . draw. . . .

"Pass. . . ."

The yells and the screams and the sudden "chunks" of men crashing into men from warm days of August until the final cold afternoons in the snow of Christmas.

It begins at the training camp. The good time. The good place. They come to us young and strong and tasting life, meeting the solid "chunks" of another hurtling body with laughter. God. It is good to be alive and be a football player. No wonder we never want to leave it.

In 1966, I picked a new defensive linebacker coach who had played both in the N.F.L. and, for two seasons, with the Patriots. After that, he became player-coach in a minor league conference and then went to work full-time for Wonder Bread in an executive capacity. I was lucky enough to have him part-time. A find. A talented man of great integrity.

Only when we announced the signing did I realize what people would say. Rommie Loudd was the first Negro coach in football. I'm stupid. I'd never even thought of it. He was just a good coaching prospect.

Training camp: I worried a little. Would anyone hurt Rommie? Would any bad words be said? It is one thing to be a player. It is quite another to be a coach.

The training tables at Andover Academy: the good days and the first contact. The first hazing. They go for it more in the N.F.L. We don't have such a raw tradition. Perhaps it comes from the six year fight just to survive. The only real hazing is making the rookies sing their team fight song or the hymn of their alma mater. Arrington was the team target:

First workout at Andover

Boston Record American—Sunday Advertiser

Sing the Notre Dame fight song.

He doesn't know it. He stands there in the dining room and stutters and sputters. Finally, a tall white southern player yells, "Well, damn it. Then sing 'Dixie.'"

Rommie Loudd covers his face with his hands and breaks into long gasps of convulsive laughter. The room joins in.

We are a team. A team. We will win it all. I know it at this moment. We are a winning team.

Later, during an exhibition in Mobile, Alabama, Rommie brought a new form of integration to the Senior Bowl. He and Richardson were far up in the spotter's booth. Someone was making too much noise behind them. A redneck. Rommie turned and said, "Will you please shut up?"

Richardson nudged Loudd as the redneck became quiet.

"Well," Jesse said, "I don't know when integration first came to Alabama, Rommie, but there's no doubt this is the highest form of it." They peered down the long sweeping steps of the bowl and continued their work on the charts.

The charts would show a long exhibition season. The Patriots' exhibition record was more impressive than usual in 1966, but some still insisted that I never play to win in pre-season games. Nothing could be further from the truth. A winning habit is a winning habit. But as head coach I must give every man a chance to play and evaluate the players one by one.

At this point the winning is not as important as the knowing: knowing which backs have the courage to put their heads down and smash into the pit, storming at it, taking the crunch and the thuds and driving for the extra inch; knowing which linemen will stalk their opponents and make that final, vital move with a tongue hanging out and a brain which seems full of clotting, sweating gauze, fighting instinctively against the exhaustion.

You find out in the exhibitions. Either they have it or they don't.

If they don't then the equipment manager stops by their lockers: "Mike wants to see you."

Some teams call it "the time of the Turk." Some coaches send an assistant to speak the bad words. One team had a system where before practice the man would approach his locker and his clothes wouldn't be there. Bare. Stark. Empty. Rejected. I do it the only way I know: "Mike wants to see you."

Training is the early part of our year; the time of putting the chess pieces together.

In 1966, we had three quarterbacks. Parilli. Huarte. Billy Laird. During the off-season Atlanta offered big money for Parilli. Instead, I signed Babe to a new two year contract. There was another unspoken contract between us. If we were to lose it this year by the inches, if I were to be nickeled and dimed and die by the inches, then it would be his arm and his inches.

Laird was just a kid, willing and able to learn, reminding us very much of Unitas. His desire will make him a pro quarterback and his desire would not let him ride a bench. He made the decision to play semi-pro ball and continue the learning process. It was a good decision, one worth remarking on. No one ever learned anything being the third quarterback, sitting on a bench.

Huarte began his learning process. For Huarte it was the beginning of six hard months of always being the imitator. Week after week and game after game he would never be permitted to have the identity of John Huarte. Week after week, he was forced into the moves of Namath, Flores, Kemp, Blanda, whomever it was that the Patriots would go up against.

This, too, can be the test for the quarterback. Huarte would take his lumps this season and we knew it in the training camp. He knew it as well. When the year was over, Huarte would be well on his way to becoming a professional quarterback.

It was a good time there at the training camp. The time of first being together again. Some mistakes, certainly. My top draft choices, Arrington and Boudreaux, consistently failed to make the right moves and show desire. For them it became a matter of next season. I knew they would be cut from this year's squad. It was a hard coaching decision, but it had to be made. They would be paid—but they would not play.

Dick Felt arrived one day. An injury sidelined him in 1965. Now he was back from Utah, smiling and in shape. There are bigger names on this team now. But once he was the biggest and we owed him one. He smiled that small, shy grin of his and said, "One more year, Mike. This will be my last one."

I shook his hand. "Good, Dick, because this is the year we are going to win it."

They came in one at a time. The big and the small.

Jim Nance was down to 230 pounds and was confident. His first season he simply wasn't a fullback. I called him in for the old "psych" late in 1965.

"Bo, you can't cut it at fullback. Next year I'm going to make you a tackle."

Nance's face was a study in fear and confusion. "Mike, I don't want to be a tackle. I don't want to play the line."

"Well," I said, "make up your mind. You're either a fullback or a tackle. You've got the talent for either. Decide."

Nance came to camp as a fullback and we had to teach him only one thing. He had a tendency to edge too close to the line, which didn't permit him to exercise options. We moved him a step back. The season proved he was a fullback.

One after another they arrived as the heat of August stirred. For four weeks we worked and practiced. The good time. Practice. Contact. Plays. Think. Movies. Short trips. Exhibitions.

The soft autumn days began and then————.

September.

I lay awake nights listening to the first cold rains on the old colonial eaves of our building, remembering old training camps, old faces, seeing the new ones, seeing the veterans, whom I know like sons, their strengths, their weaknesses. The proud professionals.

I counted the schedule. I knew if I lost only four of the fourteen games then we would win it all.

The last night the rain came down more harshly. Winter began to touch the wind. Cold. The next day we worked hard in the rain and then we left to begin the year we were going to win it.

This would be the year.

It would begin in San Diego. With sunshine and laughter and the Chargers.

It is late in the fourth quarter. The game plan is shot. A few mistakes. Interceptions. Parilli comes to the sidelines.

"Got any advice, Mike?"

My mind is already looking forward to next week. I smile, "Yeah, Babe. Don't ever become a football coach."

SAN DIEGO 24, BOSTON 0

Much later, I was sitting alone in my motel room. The loss was the fault of only one man, Mike Holovak. I was responsible. It was late and I was looking toward next week at Denver. One of my giants knocked on the door.

"Mike . . . Mike. I just had to talk to you. You can trade me if you want to for drinking. But, Mike, I'm sorry. I did the best I can. I just want to play on a winner. I want to win, Mike. Will we win, Mike? Can I play this game, Mike?"

I put him to bed and forgot his name.

And we flew to Denver.

Denver didn't even get a first down in their opener. Mac Speedie was the coach, the old end from the Browns who was Otto Graham's finest receiver. A good man. The papers said that if he lost this game he would lose his job. I wondered if the papers might not say the same thing about me.

Some writers were after me to pick up Cookie Gilchrist. Denver fired him and I could only answer by laughing and remembering Speedie's description. "What kind of a player is Cookie Gilchrist? Well, he's just like any other fullback who has a gold Cadillac with a gold telephone in it. When I got rid of him I thought my Christmas present came early."

I explained very carefully that Nance was the best fullback in the league, better than Gilchrist. Everybody laughed.

And we went out on the hot day to play at Denver that Sunday afternoon.

(Step inside my mind now. Maybe you watched it on TV that day. This is what I thought. The action on our first series in the first quarter):

Parilli throws to Colclough and we move to the 18. 65 yards. Beautiful. And sit there. Cappelletti comes in to kick the field goal. He misses. What's the matter, Gino? Does Keith Lincoln still have your kicking shoe?

We begin again, following the game plan, and reach the 35. No farther. Parilli is hurrying, throwing off the wrong foot. I tell myself that he is a slow starter. He always starts a game slow. He always starts a season slow. He is not too old. Please, Babe. For the love of God, Babe, don't just get mad and lay the ball out there. Throw. Throw like you used to. Throw, Babe.

Nothing.

Cappelletti finally kicks one from the 40. He comes back all smiles. He is three points on the way to another scoring championship. He is producing as a pro should. We're leading and hold on our 16. Our ball. First down. Parilli hands off to Nance on the buck. Nance knees the ball into a fumble. Denver recovers.

Okay, coach. What do you say now? I wipe my lips and move down the line a little bit. I will say nothing to Nance.

Denver doesn't make a first down, but they make a field goal, and we are tied 3-3.

So we try again. Parilli throws the long one to Cappelletti. The 34 scissors. It works. Gino is clear. Some bum reaches up and just touches it with a finger and the ball is intercepted . . . agh . . . I will die here in Denver. The inches will kill me. All season long I will be nickeled and dimed to death by inches. Defense. Okay, defense. Hold it for us. Get us back the ball. Denver makes its initial first down of the year. Then they try a pass and Ron Hall intercepts and goes 87 yards to the other 8 as the first quarter ends.

They are changing sides and I think, this is a national television game. God, I can see the dials flicking off all over the country.

Held again, but Gino kicks the field goal, 6-3. The only break I have going is that Denver's quarterbacks are not having a great game.

At least Parilli never panics.

Or connects.

The second quarter: In the final 37 seconds McCormick connects with Scarpito for a touchdown. Denver leads, 10-6.

We come right back, but the inches are going against us. A missed pass. A dropped pass. Finally with 5 seconds remaining in the half, Gino kicks another field goal. 10-9.

We walk off the field. Denver has chutes. Ours is marked "Chute 2." Underneath it says "Visitor's Corral." Maybe they have an extra lariat for this rodeo. I will hang myself.

The game plan. Few changes. We will stick with it. Back again. But now the team is coming alive. The defense is working. Antwine. Hunt. Dee. Eisenhauer. The front four. They are cutting McCormick down. The Babe is running the team now. Flare pass. Flip. Rip. Inside the 4.

Now, Nance. Throw them off.

Parilli has established the throwing pattern. Now he goes to the ground. Nance for half a yard off right tackle. Some old quarterbacks will use a fullback right back from left to right. Nance to the right now? No, they key on him and Parilli anticipates it and gives to Garron and he slices through the same right tackle hole.

Touchdown!

Our first touchdown of the year. It required 102 minutes and 29 seconds. Is this the year we will win it?

But we did win the first one. From that first touchdown everything went right. The sun was shining and we won it solid and 17,000 people in the stands were booing and we were laughing as we went into Chute 2 and flew home.

Mac Speedie was let go the next morning.

BOSTON 24, DENVER 10

Now we came back to Fenway Park for our first home game, playing Kansas City. Sizing up Kansas City we knew one thing—Hank Stram would go with Lenny Dawson's passes. It had taken years for this team to jell, but now Stram had the horses. They were big and powerful.

And we could beat them.

Our practice sessions were good. Tempers were on edge, but that's a good sign with the pros. Eisenhauer was practicing with a broken wrist. Before a regular game, Bill Bates must wrap the cast in foam rubber and the referee checks to make sure. But it was still a solid, flailing weapon in the infighting of the giants.

We didn't bother with the foam rubber in practice and suddenly the cast was making solid noises against a helmet. Karl Singer, a rookie, had made the team as an offensive tackle and he and Ike tangled and were fighting. Ike was swinging the cast as though it were an axe.

Chop. Chunk. Chank.

It rattled around Singer's helmet, his pads, his ribs. Singer struck back and a coach yelled, "Hey . . . Singer . . . watch out for Larry's wrist."

By the time we separated them half the team was broken up with laughter. For the rest of the week we had a catch phrase, a team slogan: "Hey . . . watch out for Larry's wrist."

I threatened them both with fines, but inside I was laughing, too. The rookie wanted to fight and the old pro wanted to fight. We were edgy. But we were a team.

It lasted until 0:57 of the first quarter when Dawson passed 31 yards to Burford for a touchdown. On our first offensive series Parilli's pass was intercepted and Robinson went 28

yards for another touchdown. There had been just two minutes before the home folks and we were losing, 14-0. They
were booing.

Finally, we uncorked one on a play Romeo had been practicing all week. He broke past the defense and was running
for daylight. There was no one in front of him. Parilli's pass
just touched his fingers. And fell to the ground. The inches
were killing us.

So we tried again. Our center, Jon Morris, was injured,
and I recalled Joe Avezzano, whom I originally let go after
training camp. At San Diego his fingernails were too long
and he cut Parilli's hands on the snap. Now, he was centering
on our 20 and Fraser was back to kick. The ball sailed
towards him, flopping and flapping. Fraser dropped it. The
Chiefs recovered and kicked a field goal to make it 17-0 as the
first quarter ended.

What makes a team? Right now, at this point. This was the
exact moment when the Patriots became a challenger for the
championship. The fans were catcalling, but Parilli stepped
over the ball and worked that team like a chess master. Pass.
Nance. Pass. Nance. Pass and rush. Pass and rush. Down to
the three and then the Babe broke out and scrambled, carrying the ball open in his right hand and running for it and
you could see it coming and we were yelling:

"Cover, cover, cover, pull it in, Babe, why can't you ever
teach a quarterback not to run with the ball held out? Pull it
in, Babe!"

Crunch.

Fumble.

But Garron recovered and Nance scored and they came
right back again and Nance scored another and at the half we
had Kansas City ragged and were losing only 17-14. It was a
rough ball game. One of the vicious ones. Hard contact. But
at half time we knew we could win it now.

It stayed tight and tough through the third period. They
were leading only 23-21 and in the fourth quarter Eisenhauer had a clear shot at Dawson and was going for him.

Suddenly, Ike's leg went from under him. We carried him off. The last momentum went with him. We were worn out. In the final two minutes Dawson scored two more touchdowns.

There was a vast sea of silence as we left the field.

KANSAS CITY 43, BOSTON 24

The silence lasted all week. The schoolboy stadium where we train was silent, damp and gray in the afternoons and evenings with only the flickering movies of the next opponent and the hushed voices of the coaches. The scurry of a water rat from the ocean. A jet leaving the airpot, screeching overhead. Ghosts and flickering images. The phone seldom rang. Nobody loves a loser. September was a bad month.

Monday, I sent Dello Russo to get Avezzano: "Mike wants to see you."

The door swung. Avezzano was gone. He was bitter. He thought he should have held me up for a no-cut contract. Better still, he should have cut his fingernails. It isn't pleasant to release a player.

The next game was at home against New York. The Jets had won five straight and everyone was saying it was their year. Joe Willie Namath was the toast of New York. But around the league we knew differently. Coach Weeb Ewbank knew it too. So did Joe Willie.

This would be the Sunday that the Jets' chances for it would end. From here their season would be all downhill.

Joe Willie came to town dressed for the action, carrying a paper bag with his tooth brush and razor and wearing yellow Bermuda shorts and sandals. Beautiful. At least he's an individual. But an individual who could be beaten:

It is a rough one from the start. Jockeying between the benches. Yelling at the linesman: "Hey—that's illegal formation . . . damn it . . . watch it . . . for Lord's sake. . . ."

"Holovak, you stink," they are yelling from their bench, which is alongside ours. Our ball first. I look over and see Joe Willie, my Pennsylvania friend with the Alabama accent. He spits and picks up an ear phone from Taliffero and listens.

I think, Okay. Watch this, Weeb.

Cappelletti has been complaining that Parilli won't throw to him. "I'm not the quarterback, Gino. Complain to him."

Gino doesn't. But in this game he is going to get passes. Parilli hits him on the 9. Gino comes off with that stoic look of his. But his eyes are smiling. He is a long way from the broken-down kid who came along for the ride in 1960. He is an M.V.P., a scoring champion. He is a tiger for the money. The tiger is riding in his eyes now. Parilli hits Colclough.

Parilli hits Gino again. Colclough. Gino. We are on the five. They key on Nance. The game plan. Let them key on Nance. Garron slithers right through the hole.

Touchdown!

Joe Willie is 1-for-9 in the first quarter. The fans are hot. They are yelling. Booing Joe Willie. Booing the Jets. The Jets are yelling back and a voice from the stands says, "Aw, sit down, bum."

Namath throws and Hall intercepts. Joe Willie walks past our bench coming back. He stops at the end of his bench by Don Maynard and says to his end, "Did you see that?" Joe Willie is offended.

Class. A touch of it. A touch of the good quarterback.

No gains; interception; Jets miss a field goal; finally, our ball on the 2. We move 9 yards in three downs. Fourth and half a foot. The fans yell, "Go for it, Mike."

Are you kidding me? On my own 12. This early? Fraser kicks badly out to the 37. The inches again. One more inch gives me the first down. They'll come at me now. They'll storm at me. They do. But they only get to the 30. Fourth down. Field goal. Bad pass from center. Fumble. We have them.

And miss.

Johnson picks up the ball and sneaks to the 27. My defense is tiring now. A whole brand new set of downs. Figures. Snell, on right tackle, 12. Mathis, minus one. Pass, pass, pass. No chance. Namath to Sauer for 11. The sonovagun could throw it through a clothes hanger. Snell 4 yards, touchdown. Snell again—is that the guy Weeb was going to make a halfback so Nance could play fullback? Hah!

We both blow runs at it. Time is running out on the half. On the Jets' 49. We struggle down to the 10, dead weight.

Penalties. Beautiful. "Thanks very much, ref. Beautiful. Why don't you just give them the ball?"

Harassment.

But we get to the 10, and Gino kicks it. The half ends, 10-7.

Championship, Weeb? Not this year, Weeb. The bounces are running for us.

Maybe. During the half, we changed a few plays in the game plan. Some receivers had better ideas. This is where the coach and the quarterback come in. A receiver will return to the huddle and say, "Babe, if I move to the right instead of the left I'm open and I beat this guy." If Babe listens, we lose. The receiver in his emotion and desire doesn't understand that when he moves to the other position or the other pattern he may change the whole defense.

Same thing in the dressing room. They wanted to talk about changes. We huddled at the blackboard and made some. The 49 would work. The flare. But one player kept talking to the Babe. Then he followed me over to the other side of the room. "Mike, if we just use the 34 instead. . . ."

"No, darn it. No. Now do what I said."

Tough. But a time to be hard.

The plays worked. Parilli to Cappelletti; touchdown! We led, 17-7. Hennessey intercepted on the Jets' 20. Garron over right tackle for 5. Nance, 1. Garron, on the same right tackle play, got the touchdown. 24-7. The Babe walked off the field smiling at me. Grinning.

The stands were going wild. Here, on national television, we were breaking the Namath myth.

But it didn't break quite that easily. Joe Willie came swaggering off the field and yelled over to me, "Three touchdowns, Mike. Three touchdowns. I got 'em."

All we needed in that whole fourth quarter was one first down. Our defense was exhausted and I prayed, "Rest them, please, offense, rest them, get us just one first down."

They just couldn't make it and New York and Namath came roaring back, reeling off 62 yards and a touchdown on a screen pass from Namath to Snell. Behind us the fans were yelling at Namath as he walked off swinging his helmet in his right hand. He looked up at them and yelled, "Yah . . . yah . . . ————you."

Joe Willie wasn't quitting. We kept trying and kept failing, missing a field goal and missing the first downs by the inches. Namath passed to Lammons for another touchdown and now we only led 24-21. We failed again and they missed a field goal and the big welling hope was that maybe we would make it after all. The fans had a new target now, Holovak, and they were yelling at me, providing that marvelous advice as if I were a blind man out there. "Don't sit on it, Holovak," they yelled. "Stop playing it safe." I wasn't sitting on it. We just weren't getting the first down and with 32 seconds remaining Namath hitch-passed, screen-passed and look-in-passed to our 9, then fumbled, losing 2. On the last down, Turner kicked the field goal that tied it. They booed us as we left, yelled at us for sitting on it. We didn't sit on it. They sat us on it. "Boo . . . bench Parilli . . . use Huarte . . . boo."

But we were supposed to lose. At least we got the tie. The Jets would not win a championship this year.

BOSTON 24, JETS 24

And so we went to Buffalo. And beat them 20-10.

Came back and Larry Garron scored three touchdowns and

we beat San Diego 35-17. Suddenly we were only half a game behind the Jets in the standings.

Then Oakland, winning 24-21 on Shonta's last minute interception.

Gambling now. At just the right moments. Sometimes taking the chance on the fourth down and a half a foot situation. Not often, but just enough to keep them honest. Picking up the speed now and moving into position.

After the Jets game I recall sitting at the schoolboy stadium. I said, "I'll probably be saying this after we lose six more games. But I'm convinced this team is beginning to jell. This is the year we're going to win it."

At last we were rolling. Doing every single thing right. Eating them up. Psyching them.

And then it rained.

Against Denver, November 6, at Fenway Park; the eighth game. Nance had a shoulder injury. We decided to take it easy on him. Denver would key on big "Bo" anyway, especially in the rain. Let them. We'd use Parilli's arm. The game plan changed because of the rain. Nance was still the decoy, but no one was going to do too much in that northeaster. Ray Malavasi was coaching Denver now. Good coach. Just holding the job open for the season—a job Saban would take for $500,000 and a ten year contract later on—but Malavasi and Doak Walker could move these guys a little, appeal to their pride.

I took only one chance in this game. Practically no one realized it was one of the few times we ever did it. There were twelve fumbles, or something like that.

We fumbled on the Denver 24, 26, 38. Gino's field goal from the 34 was blocked. Beautiful————beautiful. Who can you blame for that in a howling northeaster?

Good coaching got a touchdown: Jim Lee Hunt scooped up a fumble on the 9 and slid into the end zone. Gino kicked. 7-0. Gary Kroner kicked one 38 yards for them. 7-3.

Third quarter. It was fourth and inches on our own 21. We had a play set for it. We might have made it. Who will ever know? The ball squished from Morris to Parilli to the mud. Parilli fell on it. Denver's ball and how could they miss the score? They didn't and led, 10-7.

Okay, smart guys. Everyone who ever said we didn't gamble enough. How do you like that one?

The Pats didn't quit. The defense hacked at them. Houston Antwine picked off a fumble on the Denver 35. Gino kicked a field goal four plays later from the 36—this was a game plan? Minus 1 yard on three plays?—and it was tied, 10-10.

We tried for more: to the 31, field goal; miss; drive to the 20; field goal; miss again; and on that one there were 16 seconds left in the game.

What does a coach think at that moment?

I hoped. Very logically thought, "Look. Denver is the poorest team in the league. They're only playing for next year's coach and pay check. They have absolutely nothing to lose. They have to throw the long one. We'll play for the tie. It won't hurt us in the standing. Just knock down the pass."

Simple.

And the rain came down.

And rookie quarterback Max Chobian—he must have been the only one left with dry hands—came in and threw the thing 65 yards to Al Denson. Denson didn't have a chance on it. It never was going to connect. Chuck Shonta had him covered. The ball came down through the rain, flogging against it, swaying, flickering drops. Shonta thought he could grab it and be clear, running for the winning touchdown, and Ron Hall, floating at safety, started in to block. The ball hit Chuck's shoulder pads and bounced in the air. Denson put his hands out and was all alone and ran for the touchdown. It was the most impossible touchdown in the history of football. But it was a touchdown.

DENVER 17, BOSTON 10.

All day Monday I ran that movie. It could not possibly have happened. It did. I threw the film in the can. I tried to forget about it. What else could I do? Buffalo was back in first place and we were chasing again.

Pros unemotional? Shonta's wife had their first baby the day before the game. At noontime, he was in the locker room passing out cigars and laughing. Our friend "Tonto," the Indian.

Four hours later, he was sitting there asking, "Why me?" Rommie Loudd talked to him. Eisenhauer put his arm around him and walked him into the shower. They came out into the floor, pools of mud and soap and sweat, and Tonto's eyes were red. "Why me? Why me? Why did I let Mike down?"

Simple, Tonto. Look back to the fourth and inch situation on our 21. I gambled and lost it there.

It was just a case of the inches and the bounces. You can put all the years of your life into this game, but you have to know one thing. Up in the stands they may be measuring it by yards. But this is the game of inches.

I sat in the mausoleum amid the gray bricks. The jets took off. The water rats scurried. The rain fell. I ran the movies over and over again. The ball is thrown. It is in the air. Shonta moves in to catch it. It bounces off him. Touchdown.

Finally, I got up and forgot about it.

The problem was—would they forget it? They came in from the first practice, but they still had their heads down. Morris threw his dirty socks in the barrel and yelled, "This is the quietest morgue I've ever seen."

It was. I let them ease along in despair all day Tuesday, letting them fight their way out of it themselves. Wednesday we gave the game plan for Houston. "Okay, now. Forget it. I said forget it. I mean it. Forget it. Houston. That's the name of the game."

Houston.

We had to win this one and win it big. Shonta looked more confident. So did Artie Graham. Shonta went hunting Monday and killed two rabbits. Both of them had rabbits' feet taped inside their socks. How could we lose?

Lemm was back with Houston. Old friend Wally. I hoped I would beat him 50-0.

All week long Cappelletti had his head down.

"Forget it, Gino. Forget it. So you missed one."

But he was worried. It is like a golfer missing a big putt. He was worrying about the "psych."

I was worrying about Houston. Lemm was putting something into them. He had all kinds of problems with a quarterback, Trull, who was a strange one, and a team which was disorganized, but we knew one thing—Wally could get a game out of them. Wally could put us in a lot of trouble.

"Nothing comes easy to us," the players said. "Anything can happen to us."

We spent the week practicing and watching the movies. Flick, click, flick, click. I kept watching and watching and then it came to us. Their safetyman, Jim Norton, would cover our tight end, Whalen. Whalen was much faster. He could beat Norton. I thought, "Where did I learn this? Against Paul Christman a thousand games ago? No matter. The play will work."

We put it in the game plan.

At 3:18 of the first quarter, Parilli threw one 32 yards to Whalen. He had three steps on Norton. He was gone for the touchdown. It was the first touchdown of his professional career and he wasn't scared anymore. He came back to the bench laughing, jumping, gleeful. Now he was a professional end.

Trull brought Houston right back to a tie, 7-7, and it dissolved into the second period. We were stalled on the 28 and I called for a field goal. Parilli hunched for the ball, looked up and said to Capelletti, "Forget last week, Gino, just make sure you kick this one."

Cappelletti said, "Thanks a lot."

The ball was snapped and he kicked it straight and true and we led, 10-7, and Gino's worry about the "psych" was gone for good.

Later, he kicked another from the 44 and caught a touchdown pass. Houston kept pressing and scored again late, with just two minutes to go. We were leading only 27-21 and Houston had the ball again. Finally, there were absolutely no

Capelletti catches a touchdown pass in the game we had to win—and did

seconds left and Trull was throwing it long, long, long—*I see the ball; I can't see my safetyman, oh my God, are we going to lose another one?*—and then Henessey put a hand on it and knocked it away.

We were running for the tunnel. I waved at Lemm. "See you, Wally." We gave the game ball to Jimmy Hunt. The front four was really beginning to jell. Cappelletti was smiling. Now he was getting the points we paid him for, that the team depended on him for. Denver was a long time ago. Now we had a shot at Buffalo and the title.

BOSTON 27, HOUSTON 21

Then we went on the road. Out to Kansas City, counting the wounded—Addison, Oakes, Eisenhauer, all sidelined. Buoniconti with a broken rib, but no question about his playing. Nick is the kind who always plays.

I leave all these decisions to the doctor, Joe Dorgan, who is an exceptional surgeon, and to our team trainer, Bill Bates, who has a degree in physiotherapy. They made the decisions and simply tell me, "Eisenhauer can't play today, Buoniconti can." I know no more than that and I rely on their judgment. Football is a rough and brutal sport. There is a line on the game programs at Fenway Park. It read: "Ambulance courtesy Fallon Service."

Maybe that tells you a lot about our game.

Anyway, there we were getting ready for Kansas City. I knew I could beat Stram. I felt it, hard and cold and true. And I felt something else nagging at me. I was making an emotional mistake. There were three older players on the squad and they weren't a strength anymore. They were a weakness. I should have cut them and brought men up from the taxi squad. But they had been with me a long time and they were doing the best they could.

I sat in the schoolboy stadium on Monday watching the films and thinking, thinking, thinking:

I can't do it. I can't cut them now. They will play. They

will know ,and I will know that it is their last season. After the year is over I will call them in and talk to them. I will tell them right away so they won't hang on, hoping for another year, so that they can made a deal with another team if they can.

They will smile and shake hands and say, "Thanks, Mike," and their hearts will be broken, but they will put their heads up and walk off like men.

But this season—for all the other seasons—they are entitled to the chance. This is the year we will win it. And they will be part of it.

It was a bad decision and can be counted up as a coaching lesson, one worth more than passing notice. Never let your emotions rule your brain, not in professional football. It was exactly the right move to cut the bonus boys, Arrington and Boudreaux. I couldn't in honesty have faced the other forty men of our team if I cheated them out of a single chance to win. I had to surround them only with the men who would have the absolute desire. But now I let a lingering emotion from the old days guide me.

Later, this game with Kansas City would be called the greatest game in the history of the American Football League.

But it could be summed up at the outset by my own emotion. Kansas City led, 3-0, and late in the first quarter Yewcic went back to punt on a fourth down situation. The ball was snapped and came back slowly and K.C.'s Frank Pitts came right with it, smashing in and blocking the ball with one arm and a shoulder, scooping it up with the other hand and running for a touchdown.

He ran right over one of the men I should have cut. I just stood on the sidelines shaking my head, thinking, "All he had to do was block. And he couldn't even do that well." He came back toward the sidelines and ducked far away from me and moved into a swarm of players and hid down at the other end of the bench. I just shook my head and went back to the game.

If the Boston Patriots were as good as I thought they were then now was the time to prove it. It was time to stick with the game plan, forget about the alibis and get back into it, making up that 10-0 score.

Parilli felt the same way. He ran them perfectly, using Nance as the foil and throwing out a rapier pass, then Nance as the bludgeon and slicking right back with another pass.

He hit Graham with a touchdown pass midway in the second quarter and Graham came running off the field like a kid. It had been two years since he caught a touchdown pass and, oddly, it had been on this same field. Graham had been worried and we knew it. He had been worried that he had lost his touch. Now he knew he had it again and Parilli kept flipping them at him, using him, building him up.

Parilli stepped back into the pocket and he could see K.C.'s big Bell coming at him but he stood his ground and looked him right in the eye and then threw the long one to Graham again. Graham caught it for a touchdown and we were leading, but Parilli was stretched out flat.

For a flashing moment the panic set in. I remembered the time in Houston in 1963 when the dream of the championship ended with Babe lying there saying, "They broke it off, Mike."

I yelled for Yewcic to get in and hold in the conversion for Cappelletti, But Parilli was up again now and waved Yewcic back. Gino kicked it and Babe came off slowly, half in a daze. "What's your name, fella, what's your name?" Bates asked him.

Parilli looked up through red spots around the pupils of his eyes. "George Washington," he said. "Go away. I'm fine. My head just hurts."

It was a small, quick scene. But in that one moment, in that one touchdown pass, Parilli had continued to demonstrate one thing to every other lineman in the league. He still wasn't afraid to stand there and take it, undefended, and he still could throw it for the touchdown.

He went right back out there again now and drove Boston

back into position for another field goal and Cappelletti kicked it to end the half. We led, 17-10, and there couldn't be any doubt in anyone's mind now. You have to be a team, a good team, a clutch team, to come back against Kansas City twice.

But the inches have to run for you, too, and this day the inches were running the other way. Dawson kept driving in with his bigger ends and settled for a field goal. We were still leading, 17-13.

But the defense was beginning to run down. The perfect game plan provides for a scoring offense which gives the defense time to rest. Our defense wasn't getting enough rest and I could see it dying in front of me. Yewcic was back to kick again and the Chiefs were on him so fast he couldn't, so he bluffed the kick and shoved the ball as far forward as possible in front of him. It was a smart play, but it was still K.C.'s ball and on the first shot Dawson hit Taylor for the catch of the year—or a lifetime, one of those unbelievable jobs—one finger, one hand, tipping, grabbing, falling in for a touchdown.

The inches.

Finally, we were behind again, 27-24, as Kansas City drove back down to our 13. Dawson went to his best, the end zone pass to Taylor, and Buoniconti intercepted. It was our ball on our own 20 with 2:57 remaining and the whole season hanging in the balance.

Parilli trudged out to the huddle on the Boston 15. "Okay," he said. "Don't anybody panic. Don't press. This is a brand new ball game. We might just as well have four whole quarters. Just do what I tell you from this time on."

Time: 2:57. Nance went to the 28.

Time: 2:28. Pass to Graham out of bounds on the 33.

Nance to the 36 and then a rush broke down and a pass was bobbled and missed. It was third and 7. Parilli said in the huddle, "Graham, I need these seven yards. Get it for me on the hitch-pass. And then step out of bounds and stop the clock."

Graham was no longer the scared kid who was worried about having lost his touch. His two touchdowns had given him back his ability.

"On two, break."

The ball snapped and the Babe looked, counted, stepped further back into the pocket and hit Graham on the 43. Graham stepped out of bounds.

Time: 1:50.

Now Babe gambled it all on the long bomb to Graham. It flicked off his fingers. The inches again.

So the Babe would have to do it the hard way and he did. A pass to Whalen to the other 31. Time: 1:43. All the time in the world. Four whole quarters. Another pass to Whalen to the 22 and then Nance right through the Kansas City blitz and on third down a comeback pass to Whalen with 28 seconds remaining. Whalen caught it on the 11 and fell backwards as two men dragged and fought him down. An inch forward and it was a first down. We could have run four more plays and made the touchdown. But it wasn't our inch. He was dragged backwards and it was fourth and half an inch.

Time out! Shall I gamble it all? The whole season. If we don't make it Kansas City wins it close and the whole season will be over. Field goal. That's it. Field goal. Play the percentages.

Cappelletti kicked it from the 19 with 24 seconds remaining and we flew home to Boston with a tie.

We should have won. But we were still alive.

BOSTON 27, KANSAS CITY 27

Monday the story broke about the Kansas City spy. I ignored it and wouldn't believe it. I was only interested in one thing—Miami—and all my concentration had to be centered on beating my old Bears teammate, George Wilson. His team was new and going nowhere. They had nothing to lose and could afford to throw the ball all over the place, knowing that Boston had the best front four on defense, but the worst overall passing defense in the league.

It was Wednesday, the day before Thanksgiving. I had planned on giving the team the holiday off, but I chewed out Chuck Weber because the defense was lying down on the job. "You ought to tell them, Mike," he said. I considered it. I didn't want to ruin their turkey, then I thought, "Well, they're professionals. There is no Thanksgiving for professionals."

I let them have it. "Now, go home and think about that."

The defense was somewhat better in Miami. For six straight weeks we had been on national television. Christman and Gowdy were calling the game with Kansas City the greatest in the history of the American Football League. Yeah, but ties don't count. We should have won it.

And we had to win against Miami. The only way to be sure would be to use Nance as a battering ram, use him over and over again. We did. Parilli followed the game plan perfectly and Nance set a new league rushing record. Nance would never be a tackle now.

But Miami was one of those times of the traveling wives. The team won—but we were lucky. Sometimes they played like they were in a dream. In the final four minutes Miami scored on the oldest chestnut in the book, a razzle-dazzle lateral, and came right back at us again until Hall intercepted on the final play.

I was not happy as we began to fly home.

BOSTON 20, MIAMI 14

But next week—Buffalo.

For all the marbles. The plane flew home and in my mind I was already seeing Jackie Kemp rolling out and scrambling, rolling out and passing. Buffalo, Buffalo, Buffalo. It drummed in my mind. We had to win this game.

Of course, no one thought we would. Buoniconti had hung a name on us: "the Cardiac Kids."

Around the league they thought we were an interesting team. But no one thought we would win it. But I did.

And I had a few things to laugh about, including something that happened on the last play of the first half at Miami. I took Parilli out for a breather and sent Huarte in for some experience. He gave a play of his own selection, came up over center and tried to call a check-off, forgot the sequence, missed the runner and then scrambled through an open hole for a 27 yard gain.

Beautiful. Back in Boston they all wondered why I didn't use the kid more often.

Stupid Holovak. He goes with the old man, Parilli.

I laughed some more and thought again about Buffalo. We were back home in the cold weather in three hours.

The foregoing was one part of my season. Now came the key games—with the biggest sports goal of all time at the end of it—the Super Bowl.

But we had to beat Buffalo and we would have to do it once again on national television and at Fenway Park before the largest crowd in the history of our team.

Buffalo was a 10-point favorite. Buffalo was leading the East. Only a victory over Buffalo would put us in the play-off.

Wirephotos from Buffalo showed a huge blown up check which Collier tacked on their locker room wall. Part of the "psych." It has some influence, no doubt. It read simply "$25,000," which would be the winning share in the Super Bowl.

But I knew we could win.

"We can beat Buffalo. We can beat them again."

That was my "psych."

Monday we began with the latest game films of the Bills and after the long, long day of breaking them down I went home for the first night of sleep since Saturday. It is always that way, long days and nights of tension and being unable to sleep until finally, Monday, the sleep comes good and solid and Tuesday is better and brighter.

All Monday we had watched those films and Tuesday it continued again. The defensive coaches huddled in one room and Spinney and I worked in another. The game films have no commercials, no close-ups. They are one continuous series which show all twenty-two men with a long range shot, play after play.

We sit there with a cord and a button. The play starts, stops, is reversed, starts again. Flick, flick, flick, the shadows move on the walls. We go from man to man, end to end, watching each one individually, looking for the tip-off. When he moves, why he moves, how he moves, how can he be beaten?

Kemp was the best quarterback Buffalo ever had and in this season he had all his confidence going for him. He was beautiful to watch in action, stepping up over the center, pausing, reading the defense. He would step in and look to the right and then to the left, watching for any telltale signs on which zones the defense would cover. He was watching feet and hands. The tip-offs.

At that moment I had my game plan. I knew we could beat Buffalo again. I went home to a sound sleep.

Tuesday, we began the practice. Huarte posed as Kemp. Again and again we instructed the linebackers and the safetymen, "Freeze your feet. Don't move. Don't tip off which way you're going to go. Make him guess. Make him confused."

A small thing? Perhaps. But football is made of small things. My man Webb had been victimized in the past because he moved his feet and tipped off the pattern of his zone on pass defense. This time his feet would be planted solidly. At the last second, just before the ball snapped, Webb would switch feet and run down the receiver.

Kemp is a scrambler. We had to hang him out on the line on those scrambles. A three man line would do it—Antwine, Eisenhauser, Hunt. Dee was moved back as a fourth linebacker.

Football is much like chess. Match-ups. Harassments. Lines

and rules and squares and decisions. Sucker him in and whack him. We knew they would key on Nance. Those who laughed earlier didn't find it so funny now. Nance was now the best fullback in the league.

We had to decoy with him, had to find new moves. Tuesday we worked the system out.

Wednesday, Parilli was given the game plan.

There are those who will make much of the terms—flare, rip, hitch, blitz, red-dog, all the rest—and they all have a place of identity in football. But they are just other phrases for the basic game. Look as it just as one man against another and mark it down more as instinct than as terms. There are, to be sure, certain intricacies, but they are the normal ones between men.

Parilli and Huarte began with films. First, the defenses they would most logically be running against. Then the play patterns.

Easily broken down. Short yardage. Long yardage. Inside the 30. Inside the 10. Second and 10. Third and 3.

Every coach plays a game of "psych" with his quarterback. There are certain plays which Parilli will not run. They may be the best plays in the world, but he won't use them. For the simple reason: he doesn't like them. He knows it and I know it. I have to give him options. Sometimes I will throw in a play I know he'll never use and a couple of others equally good, which he may not like but which he does not cordially detest. In a moment of stress, he will weigh the plays. Almost automatically, Parilli will use the ones he only partially dislikes. It is part of the game we play.

While complex, the game plan is composed of plays Babe knows intimately, plus one or two new ones. Much is made of the passing of the quarterback and, in truth, it requires greatness and a magnificent touch to stand there amidst the fury and pick out the receiver. But we try to help him as much as we can with basic receiving patterns. If the primary is covered, then Babe must merely lift his eyes—like flicking up a gun sight—and there is another. If that man is covered, then Babe looks to the right. A new pattern unfolds. If this is covered—then he carefully throws the ball out of bounds. There is a penalty for this, but a good quarterback in the pros disguises it all the time. Just gets it away, taking no chance in the interception. Of course, Parilli can't run any more. Kemp still had enough of his youth to scramble and a scrambler can kill you. Buffalo would know that Parilli does not run except out of wild necessity.

Too many tackles. Too many times. Too old. Besides, a quarterback should never run. Too valuable.

Some say that there is no real intention to hurt a quarterback, but remember this: the professional defensive line is taught one main violence, break through the holds of the offense, tricky holds the referees will never see, and go for the quarterback. Blind side him; hit him as hard as you can, preferably putting your helmet between his chin and his neck. Wound him. Harass him. Make him nervous. If the quarterback is passing then jump to block the ball and if you miss keep going and whack his helmet with both hands. At least he may start forgetting things. Shake him. Scare him. Chase him.

It makes it hard to find a good quarterback. It takes a rare man to stand and take it. And throw.

There were no arguments on the game plan. It was accepted and marked down. Questions were asked. Some receivers will not give dollar value. They will go for the pass, but something deep inside makes them hesitate that extra split second—an automatic self-protection—and the ball will tip their hands. Coaches and quarterbacks must let them know we are wise to it, that it can and will hurt them even more in the pocketbook than on the field. Drive them until they go all out.

In this game plan I made two changes. Joe Bellino had been a specialist on punt returns. He would also be a receiver on Sunday. Small, sure and slight. But unafraid. If we could sneak him into a sideline spot Bellino would never take his eye off the ball.

Down the hall, the defense absorbed its movies and its own game plan. The name of the game was harass Kemp and cover all receivers; make him scramble and cover his men and while he is scrambling try to hit him. Make him fumble. Make him tired.

Make that arm weigh a ton.

Our defenses are called by Buoniconti, the middle linebacker, who knows only one way to play—100 percent. But the defense is not his alone. Signals are relayed to him from the sidelines by a code system which I will not reveal and are picked up by Nick or Shonta or whomever else we designate.

The front linemen have their own signals which they make up among themselves. The slight move of a hand. The showing of a finger. The twist of a wrist so that a huge 280-pound man with his head down in a three-point position can still see exactly what is going to happen.

The defensive linemen know their job. For the first eight or nine plays they simply slash into their opponents, crush them by weight and ferocity and try to make them mad, upset them, make them think, confuse them, perhaps hurt them.

We draw the line on only one thing. No cheap shots. A cheap shot artist is not a professional football player. He is an animal who will reach out to hurt for no reason other than the pleasure of inflicting harm. The cheap shot artist does not last long. The 280-pounders have their own code of justice.

Of course, there are accidents. Buffalo's huge front four might do a lot of damage. There would be holding—new forms of holding and tearing away which can't be seen. But no eyes would be gouged; no teeth would be torn out. Part of the rules. A big part.

Mistakes can be made. Dee—who in this game would be roving as a fourth linebacker—once went for a man against the Jets. Sherman Plunkett, I think. Dee pass-rushed him, trying to stick his hand under his chin to straighten him up, missing and putting his fingers in his mouth. Crunch. The play ended, Dee picked Plunkett up. "You okay?"

Plunkett, a Pro, knew no harm was intended. "Sure. Don't worry about it." If Dee were a cheap shot artist the Jets would have been after his teeth the next play.

Conversely, the quarterbacks must just take it. They can never flinch and never show fear. Never say a word. Ignore it. Or the blitzers will be inspired and come back even harder.

There are inspirations to a team. Buffalo used the $25,000 check. The Patriots' locker room was decorated with clippings, one of which said they had come a long way without much talent, with a bunch of nothings.

"Nothings" was the slogan for the week. The chant. "You're nothings . . . nothings . . . nothings." It echoed down the corridors of the schoolboy stadium.

The week passed. Slowly. Night after night . . . and then it was Sunday morning. I went to church and then into Fenway Park at eleven o'clock, with the cold chill coming from under the concrete stands.

It was cold. Very cold.

I walked into the dressing room . . . and now my mind will describe it to you from the deepest recesses.

11:30—One final huddle with the coaches. Noises outside. The crowd. They're coming in early. The biggest crowd we've ever had. It's a long way from the old days at Braves Field. A friend reminds me that it is exactly seven years to the day since I "resigned" at Boston College. Is it an omen? I can't afford to be superstitious.

12:00—I pull on my white socks and my old football shoes. Instinctively, I sit down on the couch in the manager's office. I look at the Red Sox manager's chair behind the desk. One thing. I'm not going to sit in that chair. The poor fellows who have sat there haven't had much luck.

12:10—the dressing room is surprisingly silent. Addison and Dee came to me earlier in the week and asked to keep the team in a hotel last night. I didn't agree. I left it up to the men to do as they wished. I don't have the vaguest idea where the team spent the night. They are grown men. They must do what they want to do. No bed checks. No spies. No stories. But every game is important. They should do it for all games,

not just for one. If it were for all games I'd go along with
it.

The friends pass through. They wish me luck, but they
look like they are saying it to a man on his way to the hang-
man's noose. We are not supposed to win this game. It is
really only seven games since we were such bad losers and I
still was saying we could win it?

Are they right? Will we lose? It is too late now. We can
only try. We will not lose.

What must it be like for Collier over in the visiting team
room? What does he feel? Old Joe used to be over here with
us. Now he will try to beat us and win his first championship.
Where is Saban now? Maryland, I guess, retired to the com-
forts of college coaching. Where is Lemm? Is he in a stadium
somewhere? And Lombardi? And Leahy? This was our dressing room in the old days at Boston College. Was it really
twenty-five years ago? Where did the seasons go?

Why doesn't the time pass? Why does the clock stick there
at 12:05? Why does it take an hour to get to 12:10? Why does
it take another hour for 12:15? We have already flipped the
coin privately. We will do it again for television. We need
the early flip to check out our special teams. We are kicking
off today.

What will I say to them? I stand near the door and look out
into the room. I look at my watch. 12:25. "Okay. Special
teams out." I put on my coat and my hat and walk down the
stairs and up the ramp out of the dugout with the kickers and
the passers and the receivers. They are working in their
jerseys without shoulder pads. I watch them, looking for any
sign that may help. The stands are full and overflowing. Will
they understand if we lose? Will they know we tried? Will
they yell and scream at us in all their pent-up emotion without understanding what we are trying to do if we have to sit
on it and die by the inches like we did in the New York tie?
Can't think about it.

12:20—Back down the ramp. Take off the coat. Sit in a
corner and bite a nail. Loudd comes by. Handsome. Good-

looking. Fur hat. Velvet collar. "Time to go upstairs, Mike. Good luck." He shakes hands. Good luck to you, too, Rommie. Was it only last August you brought the highest form of integration to Mobile? How far we have come from the days of Lou Montgomery.

Jesse Richardson follows him. Big, huge, my friend the surfcaster. I wonder how he looks in hip boots fighting the Atlantic Ocean. "Marlon" Richardson, the last man in the N.F.L. to play without a face mask. I laugh a little as I remember the stories of the nine years he dominated the National Football League on defense. Jesse puts on his hat. "Good luck, Mike," he says.

Good luck, Mike? What am I, alone in this? Good luck, Jesse. Good luck, dear old Marlon with that big homely face and the disposition of a sweet elephant except when they throw a football.

Now Art Spinney is there. Tugging on his coat. One last word. Okay, Art. Old B.C. boy. Old N.F.L. boy. He played for Ewbank on the Colts. He could play for me anytime. Or coach.

"Good luck, Mike."

Yeah. Good luck, Art.

12:47—Okay, alone now. What will I say to them? Chuck Weber comes in and peels off the top of his thermal underwear. "It's warm out there."

"Yeah. Nice day."

Chuck is no stranger to championships. Big Chuck. Big, quiet, calm, good Chuck. Lucky I answered that letter he sent me asking for a job.

12:49—I look out and watch them. Parilli is sitting there. Far away. His mind is already adjusting to the war. Romeo sits on his stool, a prayer book is his hands. He is an ordained minister. What is a minister doing in this game? Let no man be hurt. Read your book, Tony. Thanks, Tony. Perhaps this is your last year—but thanks for all the years that were.

Garron sits to the right of my door. Smiling at some secret joke. Some secret song. Shy, quiet smile. What a man he must be. No one will ever know the full story of his life; no one will ever know what he has done and lost and fought for and achieved.

He looks over and winks.

Charley Long comes by, performing his regular requiem. He shakes the hand of every man on offense.

What will I tell them? Can I inspire them now? What would Leahy say? What did Leahy say in this very room? Or Cavanaugh? I can't remember.

12:50—I go sit back down in the chair. It has only taken five years for the hour to go by. I bite a thumb. Don't rush it. Do it just on time. I look out and Bellino is coming up to the tiled pillar which leads to the shower. He is wearing his helmet. He is ready. He puts his arms around the column and sags back almost in collapse as if to rid himself of his tension.

I know I am saying it out loud, but I can't stop it, throwing the words down on the floor in the empty manager's room, "This will kill me someday. I know it will kill me. I'm going to die of a heart attack. It has to happen."

Bates is offering stickum to the receivers. Checking black eye shadow for glare. Telling backs and receivers, "The handwarmers will be wrapped in a towel by the tables, just stick the hands in the towel. Right? Right? Okay, baby."

Bates. I wonder if that old bullet wound from Korea still hurts him on cold days like this? He chews a cigarette, lights it again. That is three matches he has used moving around the room and the cigarette was going all the time. Who says that trainers don't get involved? He is as much a part of this team as Parilli.

Dr. Dorgan is standing over by the trainer's room. Handsome. Smiling. He is wearing warm brown gloves. Surgeon's hands. He must protect them. I hope we will not need a surgeon this day. I wonder if he had to give any of these players novocaine. I will never know. I do not want to know. You, can push them, but you cannot hurt them. Only the doctor and the trainer must make that decision. Stay out of it.

I roll my sleeves down and walk out to the center of the room as the referee comes in and says, "Five minutes, Mike."

Five minutes to airtime. We will come out of the dugout into this world of people sitting in their living rooms, into this stadium with 40,000 people watching, into this world of violence. What can I tell them to make it better, to make them go all the way?

I fall to my knees in the center of the room. It is the accepted procedure. I slap my chest as I say my prayer. Every man is on his knees. Every man prays differently.

The silence hangs there and the prayer finishes. I stand up and reach deep to say something great and valiant, words for the coaches' handbook, words to live by, words to be remembered.

I can only say one thing. "Just do your best, men. Just your best. You're a good team. No matter which way it goes I'm always going to be proud of you."

The silence is split and they are yelling. They are egging themselves on and now they are heading for the small door and starting down the stairs and up the ramp and I have my coat on and I am smiling. I think, "Well, it's the greatest job in the world except for the last fifteen minutes before game time. I guess if you ever lose the feeling of those minutes you shouldn't be in the game."

They are gone now. They have hurtled and jostled and pushed their way down the corridor and up towards the dugout and the last of them are moving onto the field as Chuck and I come up. The offensive team is running the gauntlet for the television cameras. "St. Jean . . . pause . . . wait to be told, Morris . . ." on and on . . . eleven players. It is 1:00 P.M. and across the country 20 million people will be watching.

The TV sideline truck is in my way and people are saying, "Watch the cord, go around, watch out, don't get in front of the camera," and we move around it and walk across the field.

I pass second base. Huh. This is exactly where I started for the touchdown in the Georgetown game of 1941. I look down towards the outfield where the goal posts sit. Is it twenty-five years since Charlie O'Rourke ran in there for the safety?

The sidelines.

The fans. "Don't try to sit on it today, Mike . . . Go get 'em, Mike . . . Use Huarte, Mike. . . ."

I never acknowledge. But I hear. We all hear. Will they want to hang me by the fourth period? Will we run off to a thunderous silence, or to boos? Will the franchise slide away from us after all these years? One game. One game. Imagine.

Weber has the phones on. He is talking to Richardson and Loudd. Huarte has his phones. He is talking to Spinney. The ball is kicked.

It is too late now to worry. Watch! Watch! Think! Observe! Hope! Wipe a hand across the mouth. Wet lips. Pray for the inches. Oh, just let the inches run for me today. Let the bounces come my way.

This will be a control game. It is obvious from the start. We will fight it out, head to head. All week long I have told them—just don't make any mistakes. No fumbles. No interceptions.

On our first series the defense makes a thousand errors. What is this? High school football? What the hell is this? What the————is wrong with you guys? Kemp moves Buffalo from his 10 to our 11. Finally the defense holds. They kick a field goal. We are losing, 3-0.

Scattered boos. Behind me the fans are saying: "Use Haurte, Mike . . . Put some life in it."

Kemp is not going anywhere. Neither are we. Have I given them the wrong game plan? Is that it? Are we losing because I guessed wrong?

But I can see Kemp is confused. He comes from the huddle. Head up. They use colors on their check-offs. Green. That changes the play. If Kemp sees something he will green or blue, or black and give the new play.

He has a beautiful style. He is slow and deliberate. When

he calls signals, he cups his hands and calls them to the right side, and then to the left. Everyone can hear. I wish I could teach Babe that. But I can't fault Babe. He had come a long way with us. He is the quarterback.

Kemp watches Webb and Shonta and Buoniconti and Fraser. He watches their feet and he sees nothing. He can't get the tip-off and he is becoming confused. The play patterns aren't working. The touchdowns aren't coming. Our defense is chipping away at his luck. It is only a matter of time. He can feel it. I can feel it. The luck is slipping away. Antwine. Eisenhauer. Hunt. Dee. Buoniconti. Hennessey is knocking down passes. Webb is climbing up the sides of the bigger men and cutting off receivers. Shonta is covering closely.

Into the second quarter. Third and 2. On our 35. Babe is not having a good day. He can't unwind. Third and 2. This is the big one, Babe. Get the first down. The game plan calls for the 34-pick. Nance. Plus 3. Get the first down. Then we will try the passes.

Set. On three. Break. Parilli, over the ball, go Nance go— Bo go—baby *go*—best fullback in the league.

Get me those 3 yards.

Nance slashes past left guard. They grab him. Jacobs has him tight at the first down marker. Push, Bo. Get me the extra yard. Don't let me die by an inch.

Jacobs falls. Nance is still going. Three more yards.

Clarke comes at him. Nance puts his head down and knocks him out of the way.

Janik has him. Nance spins and he's away, he's falling, he puts a hand out and pushes himself up. A blur now. He is sensing, feeling, looking for a red uniform. The reds are coming around him. Midfield. Nance is a fullback. A heavy-legged fullback. He can't run all the way. They'll catch him. His legs are moving like cannons . . . thud . . . thud . . . thud . . . and he is cutting and running toward the daylight. Whalen is coming across and moving away from him. Whalen—I told you you would become a great end—sees the safetyman cut-

Boston Record American

NANCE'S TOUCHDOWN RUN (Pages 178-185)

Jim Donaway (78) gets one-handed shot at Nance after handoff from Parilli (15)

ting over and makes his move and cuts Saimes down at the 15. Nance runs with a heart attack flickering at his heels, with his chest heaving through the shoulder pads . . . thud . . . thud . . . thud . . . and touchdown.

Aha. Ha. Ha. Hey. Ho. Ha.

The 34 pick for 3 yards. For 65 yards. Oh, please, no mistakes now. Get them, defense. Get them.

I am blind out here. I have schooled and trained this team and I have done the best I can. But now I am blind. Spinney sees. And Loudd. And Richardson. They call the view down. I can only stand there and hope. Talk to Babe. Set. Right. Nance. Beautiful. Sit down, Whalen. Rest. Good job. De-

Boston Record American

Charlie Long (76) takes out Harry Jacobs (64)

Nance cuts back on Buffalo 40. Art Graham (84) moves in

fense. Hold. Get ready, offense, they are yelling. Babe moves away from me, three downs, he is coming back, with that head down trudge-swagger of his. He doesn't look up, but goes to the phones that Huarte holds out. Dee is yelling, "Get ready, defense."

Eisenhauer, chest heaving, comes up from the bench. Antwine smiles. He loves the contact. Hunt adjusts the helmet. Fraser is suddenly a grown tiger of a man. Nick says something to Weber. They go out again.

Hennessey intercepts. We try again and fail. And the time runs out.

First half. The jogging, crowded run across the field and down into the tunnel. "Great, defense . . . great . . . how to go-go, offense." Some of these men are thirty-two and thirty-three years old. Where do they get this emotion? Think, plot, figure.

They sit in front of their stalls. Loosening pads. The defense gathers to the left. Weber goes to them. Spinney is there, his coat off, ready to talk. Loudd and Richardson head towards Weber. Parilli sits quietly talking to Yewcic and Huarte.

Spinney and I talk. Okay. We can win it now, Babe. Receivers. Blackboard. We sketch out a change for the second half. Our first series on offense. Throw to Graham left. Whalen right. Then Bellino on the tight corner play. Set. Okay?

A small argument. Someone wants to put another switch in on a play. "No—damn it, no. Go with what we have."

Graham moves to take out George Saimes (26)

Boston Record American—Sunday Advertiser

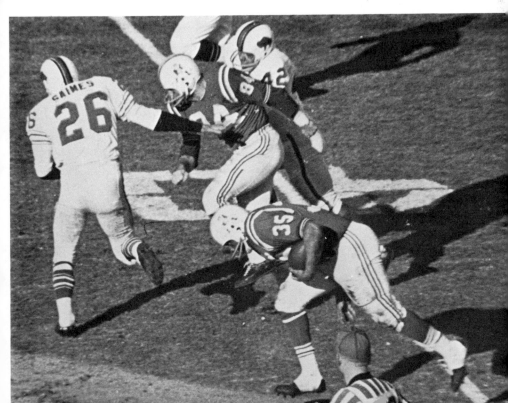

Nance picks up Graham (84), Whalen (82) and Cappelletti

I call Parilli over beside me. "Babe, you get stereotyped. Anytime you get inside the 9 you automatically roll out and pass left. Now, Babe, just this once. Roll out and run, Babe. Roll out and run. They'll split back on you. Catch up Nance for the block, follow him into the corner. Right by the flag. Roll out and run."

Parilli smiles and nods. Of them all, he was always the greatest with me. If he rolls out and throws every time I will never fault him. He is too much man.

This time we receive. Third down and 12 on the 38. Babe steps into the pocket, waits, catches Graham on the cut. Plus 37. First down on their 25.

Now, now, the Bellino pass.

I will never interfere with the way Babe calls the game once he's out there.

Boston Record American—Sunday Advertiser

Saimes knocked off stride by Whalen's (82) block at 10

But now, Babe, now, Bellino. Babe steps back again, pump fakes, head fakes, dodges. Bellino is covered, but he never takes his eye off the ball. He is a little man down there with a giant, Janik. Is this David and Goliath? Bellino can't catch it. Impossible. The ball loops out of the warm sun into the cold shade in the corner. Janik pops it off his fingers. Bellino has it and is falling at the 5. Did he catch it? I can't see. They are waving.

He got it! He got it! He got it!

Okay, Babe. Now roll out and run. Run toward the shade, old man. Run toward the corner. Set. Break. Go. But they miss a block and he is down. Up, Babe. Get up.

Second down. Garron straight into the line. On the three count.

Beautiful, Babe. How to think, Babe. Set them up.

And then he does it. A perfect piece of art, standing over the center, accepting the ball, stepping back and then suddenly rolling to the right. Buffalo fades for the pass, Nance cuts in front and the Babe is head down and going for the flag.

Run, run, run—can 3 yards be this far?—but he is slipping in there, hanging on Nance's rump and the flag is kicked over as he plummets in and . . . touchdown!

Boston Record American—Sunday Advertiser

With Byrd (42) unable to halt the fullback, Nance sprints through goal posts for TD.

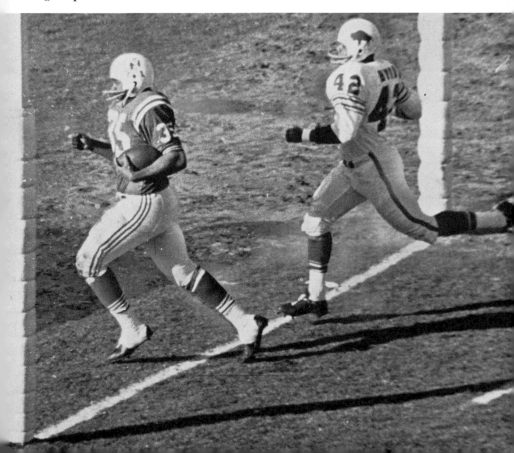

Ha! Touchdown!

That's where it ended. Later Kemp was taken off with his brains dazed. Eisenhauer starched him, catching him looking one way and caving him in from the other. Nothing cheap shot about it. Neat. Clean. But rough. Kemp was gone. And finally it was fourth down on the Buffalo 44. My mind was counting the options: Gino has a charley horse. Can he kick the field goal? Or shall I punt? No. How about delay of the game, 5 yards and then a running play? That will run the time out a lot more. They'll still be deep. They need two touchdowns. They'll never make it. Okay, let's go the delay and the run.

But Gino was standing beside me. I asked him, "Can you

The Patriots' Antwine (65) breaks up a pass attempt by Lamonica

Boston Record American—Sunday Advertiser

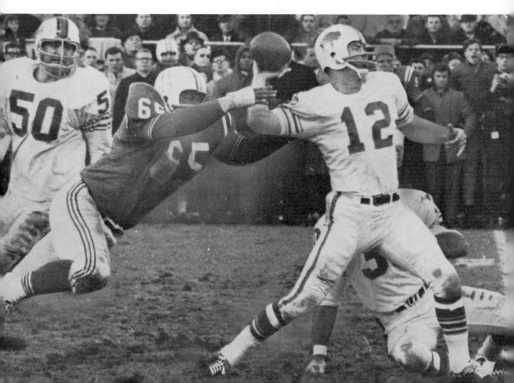

kick it?" and he nodded and I forgot my coaching dialogue with myself and ordered, "Field goal team in."

It was the worst possible choice. Gino couldn't even extend his leg and Neville was hurt much more than we knew. The Bills broke through and blocked the kick with 0.47 remaining. Now they could score and follow with an onside kick and we could blow it yet.

But you can't coach in the pros running scared. You have to stick with the percentages and learn the lessons and be lucky enough to make a mistake and get away with it.

This time we got away with it.

They weren't about to make it. Not even for a field goal, let alone two touchdowns. They were making their last tries and I was standing there with that tremendous feeling of victory welling up all inside of me, that joy of being able to stand there and watch while someone else tries to bail out in the final seconds and it won't count anyway. Buffalo was yelling for a stretcher for one of its players and the Patriots were yelling about everything and then Buoniconti was driving right through to smear the last play on our one yard line.

"You just weren't going to get in there. I made up my mind," he snarled and then he was whooping upfield and the gun was making that sharp flat sound of the blank cartridge and we were running for the tunnel.

The people were coming out of the stands after us. Thousands of them, but I felt like I was running in a vast sea of dead silence. I couldn't hear a thing; it was just a sequence of pats, rubs, shoves and bodies coming at us and the constant endeavor to stay in line and keep moving and head towards the tunnel and then get down into it as the team came yelling, screaming, laughing up the stairs into the locker room.

My team. The team. Our team. I asked for just two minutes alone with them and then we fell on our knees in peace and in silence. Addison and Dee rose first and put their heads together. The game ball? Who would they give the game ball to?

Finally, they handed it to me. I looked at it. How could it

As spectators swarm onto the field after the Patriots' victory over
Buffalo, Parilli heads for dressing room, holding on to co-author Bill
McSweeny (in Russian hat).

mean so very, very much? I would have loved more than anything in all my football life to have had that ball, but I knew
they only gave it to me because too many players deserved it.
They couldn't pick one. I walked across the room and handed
it to Don Webb. No quarterback passed on Webb. Kemp
never read his feet this day.

Now they were yelling again, chanting, "For he's a jolly
good fellow . . . for he's a jolly good fellow." They were
rubbing Webb's back and his neck and laughing and in the
manager's room all of the coaches were shaking hands and

smiling that secret grin shared among us because we knew we had done it.

I knew then the great moment of coaching. If you can help them, just a little bit, just somewhere, then you can feel part of them. Now it was their moment to laugh and yell and revel in it and now they had a chance to be champions. Never again would they be the poor downtrodden Patriots who couldn't play in the National Football League.

I looked back into the locker room at Parilli. He already had his jersey off and was sitting quietly in front of his stall. Slowly, he pulled off a shoe, then stretched and dropped the rest of his clothes and headed for the shower.

The room was mobbed. Collier was there—showing his usual touch of class—shaking hands and wishing us luck, and I thought how bitter it must be. Over in his room, the facsimile of that $25,000 check still hung. But now it seemed empty, a tasteless joke.

Bates came to the door and said, "Mike . . . Neville." Neville was lying on a stretcher with a concussion and I suddenly felt empty and defeated. What could I say to him? What would he hear? I could only pat him on the shoulder as they wheeled him by.

The questions and the shouts and the laughter went on and the coaches came by and asked, "9:30, Mike?"

I said, "9:30, 10:00. Whenever you're ready. I'll be there early."

The coaches were gone and the players were alone, still breathing deeply of their day. Ours would come tomorrow at 9:30. Then we would start planning for Houston.

BOSTON 14, BUFFALO 3.

By Monday the papers carried stories that we could beat Green Bay in the Super Bowl. *Sports Illustrated* treated us to a cover article which said we were the Cinderella team. All of a sudden it was our league and our year.

At 9:30 A.M. we began flicking the latest game films of Houston, knowing that Lemm would do everything he could to upset us. Wednesday, Lemm announced he would go with a new quarterback, Buddy Humphrey, in an attempt to settle some of his many, many problems with this disorganization called the Oilers. Buffalo fans started to scream and rant because if we lost just one game then Buffalo would have a chance to regain the title.

Lemm answered, "I don't care about anyone but Houston. I have two games left. I have to find out if this guy can play quarterback."

It presented a problem for us, too. I had no films on Humphrey, no readings on him. I wondered as well if he could play quarterback. And I'd be playing him blind.

For one quarter Humphrey could play the game. We were trailing 0-7 and I was wiping my lips on the sidelines, thinking, "Did we come to Houston to blow it?"

But Parilli called the best game of his life, steady, sharp, pass, run, and Nance gobbled up the yards, moving his personal total to 1380—enough for a new A.F.L. record—and moving him within striking distance of Jimmy Brown's all-time record. I benched Nance after 31 minutes with the game securely won. I knew he could break the record. But I sat him down. I couldn't take a chance on having him hurt.

The Jets were next. Nance smiled. He understood. He sat there throughout the fourth quarter. Bored.

BOSTON 38, HOUSTON 14

Walking off the field I said, "See you, Wally."

"Luck, Mike."

My old friend. We never talk during the season. Just try to maim each other.

And so we went back to Boston.

Laughing. Happy.

Boston Record American—Sunday Advertiser

The Babe tells it like it is

And I sat there in the plane absolutely catatonic. Thinking ahead. One more—Joe Willie Namath and Weeb Ewbank.

One more and then we would have it made. We can beat Green Bay. We can go all the way. *This is the year we're going to win it.*

Win it!

12.

The Inches

THREE THINGS cost us the world championship.

Joe.

Willie.

Namath.

And he comes from Pennsylvania no matter what his Alabama accent says.

Hate him? No. I despise him. In a manner which can only be called respect.

There is one thing about sports—perhaps the beauty and perhaps the dread—this thing of watching a guy in action. My guy, Parilli, is a beautiful thing to watch in action. He is old and he is tired and on third down inside the 10 yard line he will roll out and throw almost every time. He is old and he can't afford one more injury. And there are only two guys in the whole league who can match each other even up for the money.

Parilli.

Joe Willie Namath.

Pennsylvanians. (Oh, why didn't either one of them—or all three of us—stay in the coal mines? Heck, I was a great grave-digger. I could plant them like it was spring, even when the dirt was so hard it was like anthracite.)

Namath will take some bad raps in pro football. They will be out to cut his knee off. He will take some bad raps in the press. They will be out to cut off another part. Joe Willie doesn't live like other people. He is young and thinks he has the tiger by the tail and he hasn't died by the inches yet. He has all his luck intact.

The day will come when Joe Willie's luck will be all gone. The day will come when the Lincoln Continental parked against the hydrant will get a tag. The night will come when the rope will be up at the Pink Pussycat. The afternoon will come when some 280-pounders will be racking him up and taking his knee off and some other young kid will be sitting on the sideline phones watching him flounder like a badly hooked fish and will laugh silently, because then it will be his turn. Perhaps it will come on an afternoon when 60,000 people will stand up in Shea Stadium and give Joe Willie the no-tomorrow razz.

At which time Joe Willie is going to stand on third down and 6 and throw the ball for a touchdown. Because in Joe Willie's league and Babe Parilli's league there never was and there never will be tomorrows. You take what you can get while you can get it and know from the very first time you go down that tunnel to the dugout stairs and out to the field that the day will come when it ends.

Not with a whimper.

Not with a shout.

Just with a lot of fat guys who couldn't take a slap in the face yelling, "Namath—you're a bum."

Quarterbacks can't be faked out. They knew going into this game that they would go out on their heels. But they use the time well.

The one brief period of time in their lives when they could stand up there and go for all the marbles with 30 million people watching and 60,000 yelling and huge, vicious, violent men yelling "Draw . . . draw . . . pass . . . pass . . . hit him . . . him . . . kill. . . ."

Standing there in the pocket picking your spot and shooting it.

Whip.

Or leaning over in the huddle with 27 seconds remaining and "On two, 34 scissors, right. Don't panic, you got me here throwing it. We have a whole game."

Namath is young, but he can be marked off against Parilli because they are alike. They have all the moxie of a man caught straying by a husband (not Parilli, Joe Willie—pardon me, Joe Willie, but Parilli doesn't have a llama rug).

They have all the chill-faced courage of those Rangers in black face climbing into the rubber raft off New Georgia.

They are thieves. They are commandos. They are hunters. They are the hunted. They are the kind who go into the bush after a wounded tiger and count it a loss of the moment if the tiger doesn't charge them from ten feet.

Good quarterbacks can't be bought for money. They are already in on the steal. They and they alone know the moments.

A Parilli leaning into a huddle with 37 seconds left and four points behind. For all the marbles. For the season. For the winter. For the future. For the questions—what happened, Babe?—and saying with chilling calm: "It's a whole new ball game. We have a whole game to play. Nobody rush. Nobody make a mistake. I'm going to take you down there to a touchdown."

Or a Joe Willie. Playing only for the night in the Pink Pussycat. Nothing at stake except his name.

"Listen. This is Joe Willie. You run. I throw."

I respect them. Football is a brutal, violent game.

They know very well that in the final split second there is no way to influence the mind of the "Moon Man" or halt the 278-pound violence of the "Strangler."

The true quarterback will come out in this next game with the Jets.

Parilli.

Joe Willie.

The old man and the young one.

In the morning they will get up. Early. With little sleep. Wander around, then go out to put their minds and coordination and bodies against the bigger men who will try to take out an eye, plant a knee, tear off the last slim cartilage which is the remainder of a leg, step on a foot, break a wrist.

The big ones come at them and they pirouette and step and try to move and get away. They go down. Hiding. In a fetal position. Cover and drop and hope that "they" don't get them.

All the while, they will put their minds and their pride against another man. Against a coach. Against a giant. Even against their own team. Pushing. Driving. Telling. Demanding. Doing it.

The legends and the barroom talk; the fans screaming through their blankets and their flasks; the dull deadness of waiting to go out when if anyone said one word he would scream; the tiredness of the final prayer; the wandering the night before, tossing and turning in the bed; the early rising and the tasteless breakfast; the cab to the field; the entering through the long tunnel; the taping and the waiting. The goodness was in the week of practice before. The flickering screens. The people moving on it. *Watch him . . . watch the deep safety. When he sets his left foot back he will always go right. Watch the option now. Give it the check-off on a 33. See it? That's the move. Beat them on that. Beat them. Break them. Humble them. Drive them. Hound them. Kill them. Play for all the money in the world. Play for all winter. Play for all your life. Play against the best there is. Be better.*

That is what this game was. The last one.

The big one.

To be played in hot blood.

It began on Sunday at 4:00 P.M. Eastern time. We had just beaten Lemm.

Now we were flying home. Nance walked up and down the aisle congratulating everybody. The team was laughing and talking. I just wanted one thing more than anything else in my life—to be alone. A photo in the dressing room made me look like a walking dead man. The caption said: "Did Mike Holovak win?"

Only I knew the truth. Mike Holovak must play Weeb

Ewbank next Saturday. If Weeb loses, then the papers say
he will need a new job. I will beat Weeb out of his job.

I walked down the aisle of the airplane.

Numb. I just wanted to sit and think, sink into a catatonic
state, lulled by the 707.

Thinking—*Ewbank, Namath. Sauer. Maynard.*

Where are they this moment? What are they thinking?

*They are playing at San Diego. It must be about the third
quarter. They are blowing a lead. The cards are running
against them. The time is running out.*

*The moment of truth is coming up next week. Six days,
Weeb. Six days. With 60,000 people plus 20 million watching. You and me, Weeb. For the money.*

*I will beat you and I will go all the way. Kansas City? I can
beat Kansas City, even with their power. Once I lost. Once I
tied. But I beat them on the key plays.*

Green Bay? I can beat Green Bay.

It was not just the Super Bowl.

It is the way to live.

To live by the grace of a pass that a man caught, the man
falling, reaching, a huge body trying to break him apart, but
holding.

Touchdown!

I wondered. Is there any way I can really teach them to
catch that pass when they know and they fear and they feel
the muscles coming at them? The answer is simple:

No.

This part of it they must do on their own. This is the one
part you cannot teach them.

Joe Willie would fight. For his reputation. For his good
name. For the right to park the car by the hydrant and the
table at the Pink Pussycat. To spend the winter laughing.

Old Weeb would fight. To make the new deal for his contract. Just because he was Ol' Weeb.

They had lost in San Diego and now they were flying back
and I wondered what he must be thinking. I found myself
laughing at some of the stories about him. Someone asked,
"Weeb, how would you know if there was a war on?"

Weeb grinned and said, "I'd look at the standings. If El Toro Marine Air Base and Quantico and Great Lakes were on top of the standings then I'd know we went to war again. Football is my war."

I laughed. We landed. And now began the long week. The films, the flickering images and the practices. Monday and Tuesday. The first practice was terrible. The thought of $25,000 stole it from us. In New York Weeb canceled his practice. I wondered what he had up his sleeve.

Everywhere else people were putting up ornaments. Carols were in the air, on the radio. In the coaches' room at the stadium it was only football. Richardson took off a rain-soaked parka and hung it up and said, "Christmas is just a word this year."

WEDNESDAY

Tommy Hennessey was scheduled to be married Sunday in Worcester. He made the plans before the season. We kidded him: "Hey, Hennessey. What are you, some kind of nut?" By Sunday we should be reviewing the Kansas City films for the playoff game.

The rains came down hard again, a cold and bitter north-easter, and the workout was long and cold and muddy, but the players were laughing as they flung mud-spattered sweat suits around the locker room. Someone said, "I'd hate to think of what it would be like if we weren't leading the league."

Rain kept dripping through the roof into the coaches' room and we kept changing the wastebasket as it filled. I said, "It's a good thing we repaired the roof this year. Last season we kept three guys on the taxi squad just to empty the bucket." The joke made all the morning papers. I was a winner. Therefore I was extra witty.

The rain and the darkness fell and I was still sitting there with the phone ringing every now and then as some friend called to wish us good luck; and I found myself still flicking movies of the Jets when suddenly I remembered that I had a date to take Edith to a Celtics game.

I rushed to the Garden still wearing old slacks and white socks and while we were watching the game I heard someone say, "Look, there's Mike Holovak. He's making $40,000 a year and he dresses like a bum."

I laughed. "Well, there's another crack in my reputation. If I win the championship, maybe they'll mark me down as an eccentric genius. Right now I'm a poorly dressed bum."

The Celtics couldn't take my mind off football. I kept speculating about their defenses and watching the hands and moves of Bill Russell, K.C. Jones and John Havlicek. I found myself daydreaming, wondering what would happen if Russell were a safetyman. I could put him right under at the base of the goal posts for field goals. Maybe he could jump and block some, especially the long ones just tapering off.

That reminded me of the old days and my mind wandered off. Once Cleveland tried to stop the Bears' T-attack by putting a linebacker on the shoulders of the middleguard. Bulldog Turner eliminated the problem by hitting the top man in a key low spot. Those were the days of football. Halas had some real wild men. Someone mentioned to George that one of his players was a real Jekyll and Hyde. "No, he isn't," George said. "One of them was a good guy."

Otto Graham at this time was trying to sign Havlicek as a receiver for the Redskins. Graham knew what he was doing. Havlicek had all the moves and I was enjoying it, half there watching him, half lost in the world of football.

Graham is smart. People forget that he was also a pro basketball player with the Rochester Royals in 1946. Besides, any coach knows that, regardless of the sport, it is a good idea to pick up a player who has the habit of winning.

THURSDAY

At breakfast Edith said, "The only way you'd pay attention to me would be if I had a jersey with a number on it."

It was the only laugh all day. I was glad that the game was on Saturday. I knew I could never make it to Sunday.

The practice was bad again. What was wrong? Were they overconfident? I leaned on them a little.

The American League All Stars were out and a lot of the team made it. Nance was Player of the Year. Parilli was Comeback Player of the Year. Cappelletti had a lock on his fourth straight scoring championship and I had been picked Coach of the Year.

So I wondered, "Then why haven't we won the title? It must be my fault. I blew it by inches back there at Kansas City, or was it Denver, or that first tie with the Jets?"

FRIDAY

And then the last practice came, with concentration on goal line plays and special team plays and, finally, we took the plane, on our way to meet Joe Willie and Weeb. On our way, at last, at last, to win it.

13.

To Finish on a Warm Afternoon

I GUESS I knew it in the morning in the motel. Early, way, way early when the first glimmer of light—what did we call it in the Navy, nautical twilight?—was coming up off Sheepshead Bay.

I knew it lying there in the bed, stretched out and afraid to sleep and afraid to breathe, knowing that in the afternoon I would have to go out there for the one hundredth game of the Boston Patriots.

I guess that was overlooked. The one hundredth game since we began as a bunch of guys held together with Band-Aids. A hundred games for Bob Dee. A hundred games for Gino Cappelletti. A hundred games for Holovak.

Of them all, I had been the luckiest. I was thinking that lying in bed. I wondered what they were thinking—the coaches and the players. Funny, two weeks ago, before Buffalo, George Sullivan said, "I have a hunch you'll beat Buffalo and Houston and lose to New York. That's the game that will kill you."

I laughed. He's Irish. How could he be a gypsy fortune teller?

But I could sense it. Deep inside. Not a fear, but a certain knowledge. I could sense it in my coaches. A couple of them had this thing. Maybe it was like the old days when we went out on the boat and would know we were coming back to the pier at Itapi and other guys would know that they were not.

It was creeping in the room with the sun. It was going to be a warm December day. The sun would shine on the field for the first half.

The sun was shining in the room. But it was a still and deadly thing.

My mind was freezing.

Is this the day I will have the heart attack? Is this the day it will end?

Buy me a winner, please.

Buy me a tie, even.

What are they thinking? What is Namath doing now? Is he up? Is he scuffing his bare feet in the soft white rug? Is he carrying the phone from one room to another, scuffing along in his shorts talking to pussycats? Or is he suffering like the rest of us?

Alone.

For this is the day of the being alone. In a crowd of 60,000 . . . in the living rooms of 20 million people.

All alone.

This is the day they pay me for.

I wondered what Ewbank was doing. Did he ever get rid of that house in the other town? That was a great coaching story. Weeb went to a new team and bought a house and the team owner told him, "If you ever have to move, Weeb, we'll take the house off your hands." Who would ever have thought Weeb would have to move? Certainly not after those great years. But he did.

You don't second-guess winners. Losers hear about it all winter long.

I wondered where Weeb lived now. Probably in New York. Someone had told me that if the Patriots were in New York they'd be the biggest story in sports. Maybe. No, thanks. The only thing New York has on Boston is the late movies.

Late movies. Better than booze.

Who hears? Just motion and sound. Who understands?

I shaved. I didn't cut my throat. Maybe I'd live through

the day. Now all I had to do was eat. Take it one step at a time. Nod my head. Say "Hello." Smile. Get by with it.

You're the coach. They expect it.

"Hello."

I'm going to throw up.

"How are you?"

I'm going to be sick.

"Lovely day."

My God, I'm gonna die.

Now I was back in the room and the phone was ringing. It would be an old friend in town for the game, just calling up to wish me good luck. I knew it would be. I played a game, letting it ring, then my mind said, "Answer it—let it ring—answer."

"Hello. How are you?—good—good—fine, fine—thanks."

And then, finally, a time to move. A short bus haul to Shea Stadium, movement in and around the locker room and then the last few minutes. The locker room was quiet. Parilli was sitting inside his stall. Surrounded by thoughts of what? I knew if I said so much as "Hello" he might jump right out of his chair.

What could I say?

I paced and waited.

I reached and hoped.

Leahy would know what to say. Lombardi talks a lot. Halas would be steaming. I said, "Okay. Just your best, men. Just your best. Your best is good enough."

We knelt for the prayer.

They were up and yelling, heading into the tunnel:

Okay. Set. Here we go. Joe Willie. Weeb. The Babe. Me. Nance into the line on third down. 2 yards and a first down on their 49. Weeb is using an eight man line. He'll key on Nance all day. Yeah. Play action to the 40. Third and a foot. Babe has been quick-counting. Now he sl-o-o-w-s it down. Their front four jumps across.

That, friends, is the mark of a pro quarterback. Draw them off.

Boston Record American—Sunday Advertiser

Namath (12) passing

The Patriots' Larry Eisenhaver attempts to block Joe Namath's pass. Namath got the pass off but it was incomplete.

Boston Record American— Sunday Advertiser

Nance on the pitchout to the 29. How do you like that one, Weeb? Thought he couldn't run outside, huh?

Babe to Gino, first down on the 21. Nance plus 4. Nance to the 13. Rack 'em up. Goodbye, Joe Willie. So long, Weeb.

Babe rolls out to his right, he's running, he's holding the ball out in that right hand . . . "No, Babe, no, pull it in."

Fumble.

Beautiful. Beautiful. Don't even talk to me.

Start again. On the Boston 41. Babe to Gino on the other 40. Babe right back to Gino on the 33. You should have picked that one up, Weeb. Usually I change my ends after every play, giving them a breather from the run. Fooled you, Weeb. Babe left to Graham on the 26; Nance slugs to the 24. Babe is watching. No one is keying on Garron. Three straight plays. Down and out, stretching the safetyman, but no play. Setting him up psychologically. The safety won't run so hard this time.

He didn't. Garron caught it on the 12 and Babe came back to Gino for the touchdown.

We had the lead, 7-0.

New York started on its 20. Boozer broke through to our 26 on the first play. Now Joe Willie gave the long count and picked up an offside to the 21.

Pass! Pass! Watch the—.

Maynard broke through on the post pattern for the touchdown and we were tied, 7-7.

So who said it would be easy? You don't beat the great ones easy.

We blew a field goal. No, we didn't blow it. The distance was 52 yards. How far can any man kick? It was a good gamble, though. They took the ball on their 20 and we matched up, playing it tight, looking for the intercepton. But now Joe Willie was moving beautifully, getting down to our 33.

Darn it. Don't you know you can't gamble on Joe Willie? He'd throw it in the devil's face.

A personal foul pushed us back to the 13. It was stupid. The pass was thrown away for no gain and they stupidly tried to rough Namath up on a wasted pass. Snell blasted his way to the 10, then to the 6 and a half. Namath would pass now, but Nick read it right, only (*No, no, no*) the officials called pass interference on the one. Boozer crossbucked right into Antwine and Buoniconti. Crunch. Boozer came right back again. Touchdown.

Two pass interference penalties and 80 yards. Now we were chasing and New York was leading, 14-7.

I wouldn't change the game plan. If we started to panic we were through.

Go with it Babe. Go with it!

Purvis led the bomb squad out to the 23, Garron picked up 1, Babe hit Graham for 7 and we struggled down to the 38 and missed a field goal.

Joe Willie swaggered back. We couldn't even get his white

shoes dirty. He zipped the passes and moved to a fourth and one inch position on our 5.

The crowd was yelling: "Go—go—go."

Beautiful. They'd yell, but Weeb would get fired if he missed and lost the game. Weeb went for the percentage, the field goal. It was like a point-blank shotgun, and New York led, 17-7.

The inches were running up . . . by a ball tipped off fingers, by half a yard less gained, by a bad bounce.

We walked into the tunnel at half time still trailing by the same score. *Say something, Holovak. Say something great. Lines to be remembered, something inspiring.*

I said, "Okay, you're a little tight out there. Defense, stop concentrating on Namath and play your game. Babe, we won't change the game plan. We have all the time in the world. Go back out there and win it for us, Babe."

A referee stuck his head in and yelled, "Five minutes, Mike." We went back up the tunnel and out into the warm afternoon and right back to letting Joe Willie and Weeb make us play their game. "Change up on him . . . beat him . . . ," but he was killing us with those hitch-passes and sideline jobs. Maynard, Snell, Mathis, then Boozer up the middle. Snell, no gain at the eight. Joe Willie went back, pump faked to Maynard and waited. Snell was crossing between Hennessey and Hall—"Close it, close it"—and Joe Willie put the ball right in Snell's palm as he passed between them. Touchdown. New York led easily, 24-7.

I shook my head and said, "Well, at least we won't be tight anymore."

Parilli didn't panic. He got it back in five plays on a touchdown pass to Whalen. Gino kicked the point. The ball hit the crossbar and fell back. Gino sat down and slammed the ground. *Beautiful. Beautiful. Now, I'll have to go for 2 points on the next touchdown.*

The inches.

New York, 24-13.

The violence was coming out now. The tempers and the

fingers and the gouges, the knees and the hands and the face mask twists.

Babe hit Graham long on their 23 and Graham was away in the clear, but one man caught him by the jersey. It didn't tear enough and he was dragged down from behind.

The———inches again.

They grounded us and then Namath started again, hitting Sauer wide. We gambled on the blitz and Namath read it. He hit Sauer again. Touchdown! Now they were ahead 31-13.

Was it the Kansas City game? Did we lose it that first day in San Diego? The day the ball bounced with Denver? The first tie with Joe Willie?

Who knows? Joe Willie was having his best day ever. With a nice loose team. Joe Willie was playing for his reputation.

We still had a whole quarter. All we needed was a tie. Just two touchdowns and a field goal. We got one with a Nance touchdown. That made it 31-19. Then Cappadona got over for the 2 points.

Now they'll wonder why I didn't play Cappadona all year.

Seven minutes remained.

Namath hit Maynard on our 25. Snell went left and it was obviously a pass. Snell caught it right in front of our bench and seemed to step out of bounds. The referee jumped to the spot. Snell kept running, smashing into two Patriots and knocking them over as he made the end zone. The referee jumped back onto the field and ran in, signaling a touchdown.

Why you dirty, rotten—what the devil is this?

But the referee had said touchdown and now the Jets led 38-21.

In the television booth Paul Christman was saying, "Well, up in Buffalo Joe Collier can put down his rosary."

Parilli still came back for another touchdown, but that only made it 38-28, and there were two minutes left. The sign on the Shea Stadium scoreboard flashed: "The New York Jets thank their fans."

The Patriots' Nick Buoniconti (85) dives over Jet tackle Winston Hill (75) to stop Matt Snell (41), Jet fullback, in third quarter.

Maybe my fans will hang me.
Thank you.
I'd appreciate the favor.
Time ran out. The chant: "Five—four—three—two—one. . . ."
It was over.
Weeb was coming across the field. I walked out to meet him. He was wearing a windbreaker and his head was down. He looked up and grinned. Weeb would be in New York for another year. We would meet again in another time and place.
I put my hand out and grinned. It was not for show. I was

smiling. He beat me. Even-up. For the marbles. We were all alone on a running, pushing field of people. The hands met. I forget what we said.

I put my fist in my coat pocket. It was all over. I walked toward the long tunnel to the dressing room. We would say the prayer now, not for victory, but just to be thankful that no one had been injured. We would answer the questions. Two miles away I could see a DC-3 leaving LaGuardia. We would catch the next shuttle to Boston. Would anyone be there? Probably not. We would be alone with a few loyal friends. Greetings are not for the losers. It would be a long ride home to Dover. It would be a long night. It would be the night of the TV set never seen and never heard. It would be the sun coming up at dawn while I sat in the chair replaying the times that I blew it. A Sunday morning and a cold shower and maybe a little work with a saw. Maybe a squirrel

Nance's touchdown

Boston Record American—Sunday Advertiser

would cry out. Maybe a blue jay would fly in the woods. The world goes on. The woods are there. The house remains solidly.

I was almost to the tunnel now and the people were putting blocks on the people as they ran towards each other to clutch at the Jets. I was all alone among 60,000 and perhaps 20 million more who were watching TV. I was only me, Holovak, the gravedigger.

I was thinking, "What can I say to this team, this band of desperate men who nearly did in the year we didn't win it?"

I knew it could only be the prayer and telling them they did the best they could. I blew it. There could be no excuses. The head coach is the only one who can lose. The players are the only ones who can win. I wondered what to say to Parilli, but I knew. Parilli would be in the shower. He may play it over again in the cold winter nights. But he will never say. If he plays it over and alone that is his privilege. He will play his own hand because he is the professional.

I was near the stairs and beside them Namath was talking with Christman before a TV camera.

I wondered how many years it had been since Christman beat me with that pass in Chicago? The tunnel loomed ahead. Oblivion, the end of it all. The defeated team. Oh, we might still get a playoff with Buffalo. But it wasn't probable. Collier was too good a coach to blow this chance.

No, I knew it was over here in the warm afternoon. The gray mausoleum at East Boston Stadium would close. The ghosts on the flickering screen would be gone for another year. . . . I was walking faster now and I heard Joe Willie say to Christman, "I even feel kind of badly beating a nice guy like Holovak. The Patriots belong in the playoffs."

I smiled and then suddenly I felt the fist still clenched in my pocket and thought, "Gee, I wish this was a gun. I'd shoot him."

As I walked down the steps I saw Joe Willie throw his helmet into the stands. It would be a big night at the Pink Pussycat.

Cappelletti and Nance:
"It was over."

Boston Record American—
Sunday Advertiser

New York 38, Boston 28

Collier watched the game on television in Buffalo. All week, he had walked the streets. No one would speak to him. "It was the strangest feeling," Joe said. "No one wanted to speak to me."

Now it was over and the screen flicked off. Joe stood up and said, "Okay. I'll see you tomorrow."

Tomorrow came rainy and snowy for the first half. Clear and cold for the second.

Saban had been announced as the new coach and general manager of Denver. It was the last game for Malavasi and Walker. They decided to start a new quarterback. I can't even remember his name.

I had no complaint. We blew it in New York. Not Buffalo.

In the third quarter McCormick was in at quarterback for

the Broncos and Buffalo was so far ahead that I turned it off and watched the National Football League game.

Buffalo won the Eastern championship, 38-21, and went on to play Kansas City.

Huh. And we beat them both times.

Epilogue

So, it ended.

With no bangs.

Without even a whimper.

The final scenes had to be gone through. Into the tunnel and up to the locker room. Parilli was sitting inside his stall. He had placed his stool deep inside the locker, as if seeking a shelter, and sat there in his sweat shirt, looking far off into somewhere.

The members of what, only three hours before, was a legion of desperate men were scattered. Cinderella was dead. There were a few shoves and pushes and scattered pats on the back and "Nice try . . . tough luck . . ." as the last of them came into the room. A helmet was thrown in self-disgust. A man put his arms around a post and staggered against it. Another threw his shoulder pads.

The door closed and we were alone.

This is what they pay me for.

The moment to be the coach. What could I say? I was alone amidst a crowd of strangers. How could I bring them back to become a team again? It was my fault. When they win ,they do it. When they lose, it must be my fault. There are no excuses.

We went a long way together. I remembered it as I moved towards the middle of the room, remembering how it was after the first three games. I remembered sitting in the grey

215

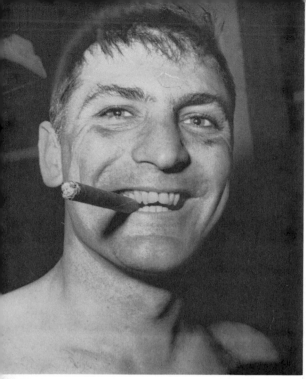

Parilli after Buffalo

Boston Record American—
Sunday Advertiser

"I dropped to my knees in the center of the room and the team knelt around me."

Boston Record American—
Sunday Advertiser

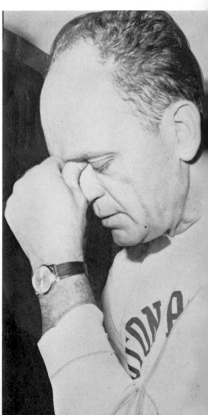

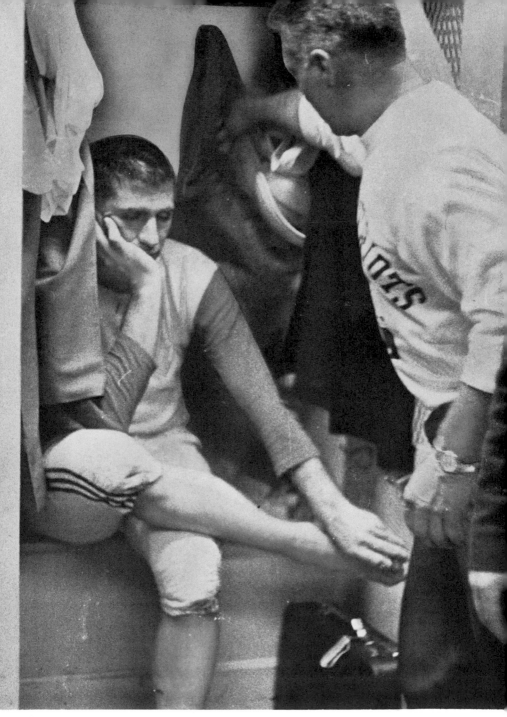

Parilli after the Jets

stone walls of the schoolboy stadium in East Boston, all alone with the projector, thinking, "No matter what happens I really believe we are going to win it all. We are going to go all the way."

Was it a fool's dream? Was it only the fantasy of a dreamer? Did I drive them too hard toward a goal I knew they could not achieve? Did I blow it all with the wrong game plan? Did I make mistakes all along?

Denver in the rain. That one last pass. Against New York at Fenway, the day we tied. Should I have gambled more?

Kansas City in the last quarter. Should I have gone for the inches on the fourth down?

I blew it for them and now I had to face them: the ones who gave it everything; the good ones who give you a thousand percent; the fakers who give you only fifty percent; the rookies who didn't make it, but who will be developed; the ones who had no next year, whom I must meet within the week to tell them they are finished.

What could I say this last time?

I dropped to my knees in the center of the room and the team knelt around me. We said the prayers. Then, I said, "You gave it everything you had. You came a long way when no one thought you could. That's all anyone could ever ask of you. The best you had. Remember that—it was the best you had."

The coaching of the 1966 Boston Patriots was finished. For the moment they were still a team; still the thundering, driving, wild, funny, intriguing, sometimes mistaken, always fascinating, group of men who wore red uniforms and were called the Boston Patriots.

Then the silence was broken. Eisenhauer shook hands with Dee. "Merry Christmas," he said.

Someone else shook hands with Tony Romeo and said, "Good-bye." Someone else yelled, "They can take those officials and," and another screamed, "Buffalo Bills—the lousy, lucky————."

I walked over and shook hands with Parilli. He looked up and said, "Poof.

"A blue Christmas.

"It was a long way for nothing, wasn't it Mike?"

I wondered what the answer could be? Was it all for nothing? Was it all just for zero? There is an answer here. But I will never know it.

For us, it would only become the year we didn't win it.

We would go home now. Christmas would be more than a word. We were going nowhere except toward Christmas. I thought, briefly, "Why does it have to happen to us?"

But then I knew. It happens because that is the way life is. You take your best shot and you hope.

You fly home, wishing you were dead. You pick up your bag and walk through the loyal crowds. The band that doesn't play. The words touch you, but don't reach you. Inside rests the certain knowledge of the interminable winter when they will ask—what happened? The knowledge that in the bars and in the clubs and in the coffee shops there are some who will be sneering and saying you were nothing. The team was never anything but a freak.

But it wasn't. It was a team of forty players, five coaches, a trainer, two equipment men, the doctors, the ball boys, the executives. It was a team of 40,000 people who paid to see it play, to castigate it and sneer at it and root with it and become joyous with it. It was the team of one city, one place, one time.

We went the long road together. We tripped on the last step. Therefore, it must be all my fault.

The long nights will begin now. The working with the saw and the hammer and cleaning up around the house. The long walks in the snow, without knowing there is snow on the ground.

The long hours of waiting for next season. I went back to the grey cell at the stadium to pick up my gear, carefully folding up the parka which read "Boston Patriots," and putting away the rubber-soled shoes. I picked up the last cans of film. Two of them were short yardage against Kansas City.

A bitter joke.

The taste of ashes.

Water was still dripping from the roof into the bucket beside the projector. "Gee," I thought. "We're sure lucky we fixed the roof. Imagine what it would have been if we hadn't."

I picked up the briefcase and the suitcase and I walked down the dark hall towards the one light bulb still going. The air was cold and sharp and the jets were leaving Logan going up, up, up, towards a somewhere I will never know.

I told myself that McKeever would be in town tomorrow. Tomorrow we would start checking draft choices, start aiming for next season. Then there was the All Star game. A lot of work to do.

I drove away from the practice field for the last time and thought, "Huh.

"Coach of the Year."

I slammed the horn in the darkness under the bridge.

"And this was the year we didn't win it."

I drove down into the tunnel and then I found myself laughing. When Bulldog Turner was playing center for the old Chicago Bears he fell out of the third floor window of a hotel party one night, right through an awning and onto the street.

Crash. Bang.

A foot cop came rushing up and asked, "What happened?"

Turner dragged himself up from the concrete and said, "I don't know. I just got here myself."

I was chuckling as I drove through the tunnel.

Pro football players.

Huh, pro football.